ANGELS, APES, AND MEN

By the same author:

ANGELS, APES, AND MEN

STANLEY L. JAKI

Sherwood Sugden & Company
PUBLISHERS
315 Fifth Street, Peru, Illinois 61354

First Printing 1984
Second Printing 1987
Third Printing 1990

ISBN 0-89385-017-9

Sherwood Sugden & Company, Publishers
315 Fifth Street
Peru, Illinois 61354

CONTENTS

PREFACE

The text of the three chapters of this book was originally presented in the form of three lectures at the Institute for Christian Studies, Toronto, in late February, 1981, as its special annual program. It is my pleasure to express my appreciation to the Trustees and Faculty of the Institute for the invitation to speak on any of the major aspects of Christian anthropology. The message and gist of these lectures is as old as the New Testament. There, in some momentous statements of the Master from Nazareth, man is spoken of as an entity that remains alive even after physical death. Upon reflecting on those statements, such as the one addressed to the good thief, Christian thinkers from the start saw man as a unity of body and soul, the very basis of Christian anthropology. The latter may appear as now being under a desperate siege, but this is not the chief concern here. Actually, the notion of man as a unity of body and soul may appear almost trouble-free when—and this is the chief concern in these lectures—a close look is taken at the ravages of inner logic which is at work when either man's body or man's soul is ignored in modern philosophical and scientific discourse. Pascal already noted that logic and spelled out in his inimitable way the results in store. In the abstract perspective of Descartes' mathematical physics man readily transformed into a mere mind—an angel of sorts. In the markedly empirical biological perspective, as articulated by Darwin, man inevitably turned into an ape. It tells something of the intrinsic nature of science that such one-sided presentations of man were to meet their rebuttal in further major scientific conquests. A signal evidence in this respect is the thinking implied in Einstein's chief achievements, or modern scientific cosmology. It has been acquired in a manner very different from the one in which angels are believed to operate, and is immensely superior to anything apes seem capable of. That man's mysterious duality has not ceased assuming new perspectives and vindications strongly suggests its being a trustworthy tenet, however traditional.

Easter, 1981   S. L. J.

"It is dangerous to make man see too clearly his equality with the brutes without showing him his greatness. It is also dangerous to make him see his greatness too clearly, apart from his vileness. It is still more dangerous to leave him in ignorance of both. But it is very advantageous to show him both. Man must not think that he is on a level either with the brutes or with the angels, nor must he be ignorant of both sides of his nature; but he must know both."

—Pascal, *Pensées* No. 418

I

FALLEN ANGEL

"The unfortunate thing is that he who would act the angel, acts the brute."

—Pascal, *Pensées* No. 358

Interview with Descartes

If asked about the Spring of 1648, probably all historians would answer with a reference to the Fall of that year. They would, as a man, recall the Peace Treaty of Münster (Westphalia) which ended, in October 1648, the Thirty-Year War, one of the most disastrous wars in history. If those soldiers and civilians who lived through 1648 could be asked, they would be found too exhausted to say much. Europe lay prostrate not only in body but in spirit as well. People everywhere seemed to have grown tired of controversies between Catholics and Protestants. The supremacy of Christian theology in European life was over. The age of Faith, the Middle Ages, had run its course.

A new age, the age of Reason, was in the offing. As is the case with new turns in history, they stand out mostly in retrospect. Some of the events which mark such turning-points make hardly a ripple when they actually take place. This is not to suggest that Descartes, who more than anyone else ushered in modern rationalism, made no stir while alive. But some momentous encounters in his life remained to be perceived only by posterity. In April 1648 Europe's attention was no longer focused on Holland, scene of major campaigns a year earlier, and much less on Egmont, a small seaside village east of Alkmaar. The heyday of the Counts of Egmont was long past. As to the village, only major encyclopedias have a line or two for it, though never with a reference to Descartes' long stay in the area. Only a few historians of philosophy would sit up on hearing the name of Frans Burman[1] whom Descartes treated there, on April 16, 1648, to a long conversation which Burman recorded in great detail.[2]

Burman was one of those many educated people who read Descartes' books and were dazzled as well as puzzled. There was indeed much dazzling in Descartes' books covering almost all fields of knowledge, from mathematics through astronomy and physics to anatomy and philosophy. Descartes was puzzling too because he claimed nothing less than that he had forged a foolproof access to all kinds of truth and secured protection against committing any major error. No philosopher until then promised so much and so sweepingly. Even Plato and Aristotle bemoaned in their own ways the persistence of errors, whatever their presumed unearthing of the philosopher's stone. It took no extraordinary intellect to see that there was something superhuman in Descartes' posture and program. Burman had, of course, to be tactful with his illustrious host. He seemed to have looked for a pretext, however inappropriate, to touch on the very core of Descartes' philosophy. The only (and incidental) reference to angels in Descartes' *Meditations on First Philosophy* hardly justified on Burman's part a specific query. It was attached to Descartes' declaration in the Third Meditation that of all ideas man could conceive of only one, the idea of God, which could not have had its origin in man himself. As regards the ideas, Descartes wrote, "which represent to me other men or animals, or angels, I can, however, easily conceive that they might be formed by an admixture of other ideas which I have of myself, of corporeal things, and of God, even although there were apart from me neither men nor animals nor angels, in all the world."[3]

In posing his query Burman conceded that with respect to the idea of angels, pure minds or spirits, "we must form it from a reflection on our mind to such an extent that we cannot, in essence, perceive anything about angels that we would not perceive to exist in our minds." But, Burman asked, "should not therefore angels and our minds be identical since both are merely thinking beings?" Descartes' answer was not only very revealing but also contradictory, a fact which Burman, in light of his question, may have very well perceived. He was hardly in a position to take to task his eminent host on such an elementary blunder. The conversation, as recorded by Burman, gives the impression of a news conference in which select questions are answered from a patently superior position. Descartes certainly felt superior, extremely superior. Unless he were willing to compromise his philosophy, he had to admit, of course, that both angels and men were thinking beings. But was Descartes justified by his philosophy in stating that angels may have many more perfections than possessed by the human mind? Indeed, he had no justification at all, a predicament which he tried to cover up with a derisory remark on Aquinas' reasoning on the various degrees of perfection among angelic intellects. "In no other respect was Thomas more preoccupied and more inept at the same time," went Descartes' verdict, which carried its own indictment. For whatever may be said of Aquinas' ineptness about angels, Descartes' few words on them were not even clever chatter. He started by contradicting himself and then sidestepped the issue: "We hardly know anything about angels, for such a knowledge [about angels] we do not derive from our minds. We are in ignorance about all that customarily is discussed about angels, namely, whether they can be united with bodies, or the characteristics of their bodies which they often assumed in the Old Testament, and the like." Burman, or anyone in his right mind and familiar with Descartes' statement about angels in the Third Meditation, could now only gasp. Burman could also see Descartes slip to a dangerous ground, the field of orthodoxy. To cover his position, Descartes urged the stance of Christian piety though not without a touch of jeer. "It is more profitable to believe details given about angels in the Scriptures, namely, that they were young or appeared to be young and the like."[4]

With a touch of jeer, without however jeering. Descartes in no way wanted to ridicule Scripture and Christian faith. Unless a devout Catholic, he would not have made a pilgrimage of a thousand or so miles to Loretto, a famed shrine of Mary. He received with great piety the last rites as he faced death in Stockholm.[5] One can safely assume that Descartes believed in angels. Belief in their existence was shared by all Christians at that time. To the question, "What are angels after all?", posed to him at dinner table, Luther's reply was firm and straight: "An angel is a spiritual creature created by God without body, for the service of Christendom and especially of the Church's ministry."[6] Calvin was categorical: "The angels are dispensers and administrators of God's beneficence toward us...they keep vigil for our safety, take upon themselves our defense, direct our ways, and take care that some harm may not befall us."[7] The dozen or so generations of Catholics raised on the Catechism of the Council of Trent would have found in these quotations nothing different from their faith.[8] As to our latest generation of Catholics, they are often treated to "theological" dicta on angels[9] which fully deserved Maritain's sharp rebuke. The fashionable dismissal of angels, he remarked, is really a tactic aimed at making Christians believe that fallen angels, especially their leader, need not be taken seriously. Whatever the state of belief in angels today among Catholics (and Protestants), if four hundred years ago there were a difference between them concerning angels it related to the broader issue of *fides quaerens intellectum*. While Catholics were urged to probe their faith rationally as much as possible, Protestants were exhorted to rely instead on faith alone.

Angel's ambition

Whatever may be said of Descartes' Catholicism, nothing would have been more natural than for the founder of Cartesianism to speculate on angels. Why did he recoil from doing so? Why did he brush off Burman's query? For answer to questions which involve patent contradictions on the part of a great mind, one has to resort not so much to logic as to psychoanalysis. Descartes did not want to speak of angels lest he reveal something of his inner conviction that he was to provide mankind and Christendom with a service befitting an angel. To promise a method securing one from errors (at least from all major ones) and to spell out infallibly all science encompassing man's body, as well as the body of stars, was a role which only angels could play. Tellingly, Descartes wanted to play such a role no sooner than he had three dreams during the night preceding the feast of St. Martin in 1618.[11] Dreams, unless directly produced by God, have natural antecedents, antecedents that are at times better kept under cover. The roots of Descartes' dream, in which he saw himself come into the possession of the very essence and method of truth, are to be sought not only in his interest in geometry, but also in the far less reputable aspirations of Rosicrucianism.[12] Disreputable as Rosicrucianism may appear today, it was one of those trends which, like its kindred versions, Hermetism and Cabbala, left few untouched during the 16th and 17th centuries. At times the result was unmitigated confusion, as shown by Bruno's discourse on scientific topics such as Copernicus' system.[13] In the case of Descartes, the appearance of rationality was carefully maintained, though only by his putting a mask on his professed aspirations. He donned the mask immediately following his famous dreams.

Less than two months after the dreams, Descartes, not yet twenty-three, began writing his "Cogitationes privatae" which started with the following statement for the first day of January, 1619: "Just as actors, who are advised against appearing on the stage with a blush on their face, put on a mask, I too enter, with a mask on, the theater of the world in which I have so far lived as a spectator."[14] Cryptic as these words may appear at first, they can be understood if one assumes that Descartes wanted to hide his view of himself as a superior man, an angel in short. He knew—he did not jettison all common sense—that he would blush were he to present himself to his fellowmen as a being far superior to them. While all this has to be conjecture, the reading of Descartes' works can leave no doubt that his claims about truth and knowledge required far greater powers than those of mere man. Those powers, as he described them, were, in fact, angelic.[15] Unfortunately for Descartes, and for posterity as well, there are two kinds of angels. One kind, which had for leader the bearer of all light, Lucifer, rushed headlong into a disastrous fall.

Speaking of Lucifer, one thinks of Michael, a name which means " who is like God." It is also a hallowed shorthand, telling perhaps less of God than of Lucifer's daring and downfall. Lucifer wanted to play God. How an angel can do that is a question for which answers, very speculative to be sure, may be found in the writings of an Aquinas or a Maritain. All such answers rest on considering angelic nature, pure intellects, whose cognition has three main features. The mode of that cognition is *intuitive*, its origin is *innate*, and its operation is *independent of things*.[16] The Cartesian theory of errorless human knowledge is expressed in exactly the same terms.[17] It should not be surprising that a man, believing himself to be capable of knowing in such a way, should try to play God. Descartes tried to do this in the only sense in which a poor mortal can do it, namely, to dictate to God how to go about the business of creation.

Descartes' apologies that he in no way prescribed to the Creator how to fashion a world out of the chaos,[18] have convinced only some Cartesians. He was the first of modern scientists who fell to the temptation in which man is lured into deriving a priori the shape, structure, and laws of the universe. The core of an a priori derivation is not that it relieves one of laborious search and experimentation (although this may reveal a good deal about the merits of the enterprise). The core is rather the consequence that once such a derivation is achieved, the possibility that God could have created any other world is pre-empted. A God who is bound by inner necessity to create the very world which exists is a poor shadow of himself. The true creator of such a universe is the man sold on a priori reasoning, a very fallible way of playing God. As one could expect, the universe fashioned in such a way is a very fallible construct, and so is its science. The science and universe of Descartes provide a perfect example.

This is not the place to recite all the debacles, big and small, of Cartesian physics and cosmology. A few examples, though, may not be amiss. Of the half-dozen rules which Descartes specified for the collision of bodies—certainly a basic subject for physics—none was correct. His all-purpose mechanistic model, the vortex motion, was found particularly inept in explaining the elliptical motion of planets, and especially the orbit of those most spectacular phenomena of the skies, the comets, of which Descartes' century witnessed unusually large specimens, and in large numbers at that. Worse, although Descartes boasted that in his physics there was nothing which was not equivalent to mathematics, nowhere in Descartes' writings on the physics of tangible material bodies could one find a mathematical formula. A genius in geometry, such as

Descartes, was not needed to notice that snowflakes, when looked at through a magnifying glass, appeared plainly geometrical. The worst of it all was Descartes' disregard of experiments. Experiments, he claimed, were never needed for establishing a basic law of physics. Such laws had to be obtained by a priori reasoning alone. Experiments could at most clarify secondary points. Thus Descartes' call to all scientists to communicate to him their experiments because he alone could properly interpret them,[19] was a reflection both on his slighting of experiments and also on his sense of being superior to his fellowmen. He certainly felt superior to Harvey, some of whose conclusions on the circulation of the blood were not good enough for him. That Descartes' achievement in biology does not amount to much may be guessed from his infatuation with the program of bringing that science to such a pitch that it would yield, if not freedom from bodily death, at least patriarchal life-span.[20] Angels must have watched in disbelief.

Ghost in the machine

Were Descartes' failure in physical science—his cosmology was soon spoken of as a mere novel[21]—but one of the many such failures, it would hardly deserve recalling. Descartes' failure is still instructive because he spelled out all the reasons for it. Those reasons are rooted in his anthropology—his wholly-mistaken notion of man. Descartes' man is a ghost in a machine, a commonplace long before Arthur Koestler published a book with that title.[22] What has been invariably disregarded is the impact of a mistaken anthropology on one's articulation of the scientific method and science. In the absence of a close look at that connection, agonizing utterances over the tragic shortcomings of Descartes' notion of man remain largely inconsequential. Miguel de Unamuno was certainly right in stating that the real defect of Descartes' method is not his resolve to doubt everything—although this is self-defeating enough. The doubting itself cannot be doubted. The defect lies in Descartes' resolve "to begin by emptying himself of himself, of Descartes the real man, the man of flesh and bone, the man who does not want to die, in order that he might be a mere thinker—that is, an abstraction."[23] As Unamuno quickly added, the real man, the real Descartes, slipped back to the scene almost immediately. This was to be expected as no man can discourse for long as if he were a disembodied spirit.

Descartes' return to the scene took place more subtly than Unamuno and others—specialists in philosophy, arts, and letters, but not in the sciences—would have us believe. Descartes' endorsements of poetry and eloquence in the *Discourse on the Method* are mere platitudes.[24] Many of his contemporaries could have spoken much better on those topics. The really significant aspect of the return to the scene of Descartes, the real man, who is not an angel but a captive of his own very human preconceptions, becomes evident in his account of the mind-body relationship. The account is dominated by his infatuation with the idea of extension. Descartes knew better, of course, than to speak of the soul as something extended or having dimensions. Fatal errors do not slip into great philosophical systems in a crude way. Yet their presence, subtle to be sure, is never remote. In the same breath in which Descartes spoke of the soul as being dimensionless, he also spoke of it as being "in *some* manner indivisible"[25] (italics added). He seemed unwilling to state categorically the indivisibility of the soul, because he was obsessed with that always-divisible spatiality which he conquered for mathematics through analytical geometry, his most enduring claim to fame. He immediately added that it is "necessary to know that although the soul is joined to the whole body, there is yet in that body a certain part in which the soul exercises its functions more particularly than in all the others."[26] Thus the soul was subordinated to spatiality and everything else which spatiality implied as a basic explanatory device. As all fatal errors, this too was just a hair's breadth removed from truth, or rather couched in something very close to the truth. Modern brain research looks for the seat of higher mental functions in much the same direction as Descartes looked for it, "not the whole brain, but merely the most inward of all its parts, situated in the middle of its substance and suspended above the [spinal] duct."[27] Being too preoccupied with spatiality, Descartes wanted to be all too specific. In his singling out the pineal gland there was something of the exactness of a geometer specifying the zero point of his co-ordinate system.

Nothing is more difficult than to speak of the brain-mind or mind-body relationship. It is a mysterious coin with two luminous sides. The only way to handle it is to follow the advice once given about a tax coin and render both mind and body their respective dues. In a sense the Thomistic doctrine of the soul as the form of the body states precisely this. It is a doctrine respecting facts, refractory though they may be to the impatience of reductionism. Lacking intellectual patience Descartes from the start read his own mind into Scholastic terms.[28] Had Descartes appreciated Thomas's doctrine of soul, he would have kept equal respect both for Thomas's emphasis on the priority of the sensory (thoroughly misunderstood by Locke and other empiricists) and for his simultaneous emphasis on the active role of the intellect *(intellectus agens)*, mistakenly viewed by many nowadays as a vote by Thomas for idealism. Both emphases could but degenerate into shibboleths of empiricism and idealism once they were no longer considered as two sides of one and the same coin. Had Descartes pondered this, he would have retained a healthy respect for the sensory and experimental. He might even have perceived that the experimental, being inexhaustible in new data, casts a pallor on purportedly definitive systems. At the same time he might even have spotted for the intellect a healthier role than an intuition of all basic truths in one fell swoop which puts an end to any further creativity. The reward for acknowledging the mysteriousness of the mind-body relationship would have been a notion of science as an open-ended enterprise with ever new challenges and exploits.

Behind the debacle which is Descartes' performance in physical science lies a disastrous bargain. He wanted the coin of truth at the price of eliminating all mystery. The transaction secured for him only his own perception of extension, or space in a broader sense, which he took for an utterly luminous, ultimate, and exhaustive verity. In more technical parlance, he bargained for Euclidean geometry, which certainly fitted man's experience of his immediate surroundings, as a universally valid expression of reality. Thus Descartes performed, long before Kant thought to have done it first, that turn which became called Copernican, although it was the very opposite of what Copernicus performed. What Copernicus did was to transform geocentrism into heliocentrism, and let heliocentrism rest on theocentrism, the best, even the only safeguard against anthropocentrism of any kind. Copernicus never tried to refashion traditional Christian anthropology, let alone to dictate to the Creator. What Descartes did was to lock human thought into an anthropocentrism which could serve only as a strait-jacket for science. Tellingly, in Descartes' cosmos God was needed, as Pascal did not fail to notice right there and then, only to perform a primordial act. It was infinitely less than the true primordial act which is creation out of nothing. The act in question was a mere fillip, to recall Pascal's characterization of it.[29] It did not even deserve to be called an act. It was a worthy forerunner of that chance quantum flip[30] in which some modern cosmologists try to locate the origin of our actual world. And, as Pascal noted, Descartes would have gladly done without it.[31]

A subtle indication of the anthropocentrism of Descartes' system can be perceived in the sway it held over a generation or two. Ever since, the history of philosophy in the Western world has been a repetition of the same pattern: the transient glory of systems—idealism, positivism, existentialism—each duly buried by its successor. In the case of Descartes' system the specific aspect of that anthropocentrism was the ease with which his discourse about cosmic evolution could be imagined. Once more anthropocentrism and shallowness went hand in hand. As modern studies on scientific creativity showed, imagination is an essential part of the process. But the imagination involved in scientific creativity has been found unfathomable, multiple in patterns, irreducible to any scheme.[31] This irreducibility reflects something of the mysteriousness of man's nature. The imagination needed for a comprehension of Descartes' system was quite different. It was nothing more than the possibility of visualizing each and every physical interaction on the small as well as on the large scale. Indeed, it was so easy to imagine Cartesian physics and cosmogony that "they could readily be grasped by women," a circumstance about which Father Malebranche felt markedly apologetic.[32] Rather, that saintly priest and the most acute among Cartesians, should have apologized for his system of occasionalism. According to it, external things are not causes of knowledge, but so many occasional or disconnected events which God creates so that the successive steps of man's knowledge may be mirrored outside him. Through this subtle abolition of externality Cartesian anthropocentrism is carried to its ultimate. Malebranche should have realized that female anthropocentrism, so evident in its imaginative power, was less intent on camouflaging itself than is usually the case with its male counterpart, all too often an inept facade.

Thinking matter

The ease with which Cartesian physics could be imagined suggests its low scientific status when compared with Newtonian physics. Newton's physics was accessible, at least in its intricate parts, only to minds tuned to the abstractions of differential geometry. To be sure, imagination was needed, but only in its kind which is synonymous with that profound cogitation in which the conscious and subconscious are in a constant interplay. Newton himself provided a clue when he credited his epoch-making feat to long and heavy concentration on the subject.[33] Clearly, he would have used a different phrase had he been convinced that all he had done was to deduce, *à la* Descartes, all the consequences of one single intuited truth, which he could grasp because it was innate in him and accessible to him with no reference to things. Newton's comment—unfortunately very brief—on the manner in which he discovered the pivotal points of his physics is all the more significant concerning its non-Cartesian character because some of Newton's dicta in the Queries of the *Opticks* on brain-mind relationship could have been taken word for word from Descartes' *Passions of the Mind*.[34] Again, had Newton been more than superficially Cartesian, it would have been most natural for him to give credit for the *Principia* not to his mind but to the apple which fell on his head. Such an impact could conceivably have activated his pineal gland just as well as could the soul attached to it. Newton then could have anticipated de la Mettrie in stating that Materialism was the true face of Cartesianism.

Had Newton noted in the *Opticks*, first published in 1704, that Cartesian philosophy gravitated towards materialism, he would not have made a first thereby. Pascal had already laid bare the inner logic of Cartesianism by noting that "he who would act the angel acts the brute."[35] While Newton could be supposed to have remained unaware of Pascal, he must have seen that logic unfolded by Locke, however unwittingly. After all, Locke's *Essay concerning Human Understanding* started with a broadside on innate ideas and truths. The mind at its inception was for Locke a *tabula rasa* ready to receive sensations as its sole nourishment. The end point of Locke's reasoning, a mind not necessarily different from matter, was just as un-Cartesian. The logic leading Locke along that route was, however, Cartesian. An all too clear proof of this is the geometrical analogy which introduces Locke's suggestion about matter capable of thinking: "We have the ideas of a *square*, a *circle*, and *equality*; and yet, perhaps, shall never be able to find a circle equal to a square, and certainly know that this is so . . . . We have the ideas of *matter* and *thinking*, but possibly shall never be able to know whether any mere material being thinks or no." For a way out of that dilemma Locke looked at revelation, without which it was "impossible for us . . . to discover whether Omnipotency has not given to some systems of matter, fitly disposed, a power to perceive and think, or else joined and fixed to matter, so disposed, a thinking immaterial substance." Mere "contemplation of our own ideas," Locke stated, was insufficient to eliminate the possibility of a thinking matter.[36]

Self-styled Newtonians

The piety of Locke was one thing, his perspicacity another. He failed to realize that reference to revelation was already losing its appeal. Locke the philosopher was particularly shortsighted on two consequences of his anthropology in which sensations were not balanced with a proper role befitting the intellect. One consequence was Hume's sensationism and scepticism, coupled with a thinly-disguised materialism and atheism. Another consequence was a poor grasp of science evidencing little or no uneasiness. Locke became a forerunner of Hume also in the latter's misconstruction of science, of Newton's science, to be specific. Unlike Hume, Locke at least was honest about his inability to read the *Principia*. He sought and received assurance from Huygens that all propositions there were true. Locke's resort to Huygens was no secret in Newton's entourage. Indeed it was recorded for posterity by Desaguliers, a confidant of Newton. Desaguliers' account of the story is instructive not only about Locke, but also about the empiricism in light of which Newton's accomplishments began to be viewed by some in his circle, to say nothing of most of those outside it, such as the *philosophes*.

As to Locke, the account reveals the naiveté of a philosopher confident of becoming a trustworthy interpreter of physics, without being able to read its great classics. Being reassured by Huygens about the dependability of all of Newton's propositions, Locke "took them for granted and having carefully examined the Reasonings and *Corollaries* drawn from them, became a Master of all the Physics." The reasonings and corollaries had to be of Locke, not of Newton, because the corollaries in the *Principia* were not less mathematical than the propositions and therefore inaccessible to Locke. The account revealed something also of Desaguliers' miscomprehension of Newton's philosophy. He started his description of it as follows: "Tho' its truth is supported by Mathematicks, yet its Physical Discoveries may be communicated without."[37] The second part of the statement was largely true. Most of Newton's discoveries could be visualized, the very thing demanded by empiricism. The first part was less than half true. The discoveries of Newton were not merely supported by mathematics, they were generated to a large extent by mathematics and in particular by that infinitesimal calculus of which Newton was a co-discoverer. It was not the first time that mathematics generated physical discoveries, and brought witness to the role of the mind. Each time a rebuttal was served on empiricism and its anthropology because they leave no room for a mind, which is not *only* a *tabula rasa* but also an *intellectus agens* able to find in the sensory more than mere matter. The truth of the insight of the Greeks of old, that mathematics reveals a divine spark or at least something supra-material in man, received further confirmation as new chapters opened in mathematics and in its use by physics.

In tracing Western intellectual development from Descartes to Locke and beyond, the steps to be followed are so customary as to be almost platitudinous. All too often platitudes are born of intellectual laziness which in time acquires an insuperable inertia. Since no less a figure than Newton stands at midpoint in that development it has become imperative to look at the great 18th-century philosophers as having worked under the influence of Newton. Most historians of modern philosophy, responsible for that imperative, have given, however, no evidence of having studied Newton's *Principia.* This is why they failed to be struck by the extremely weak evidence provided by Hume and Kant concerning their grasp of Newtonian physics. Both had at best a veneer of information about it, to say nothing of its vehicle, infinitesimal calculus. Without acquiring a solid scientific formation, and without being the kinds of geniuses who, like Johann Heinrich Lambert, could instruct themselves in the highest branches of mathematical disciplines,[38] Hume and Kant curiously wanted to make first a name for themselves with writings on science.[39] As could be expected, both were dismal failures in that respect and they could not help suspecting this. Partly because of this they turned toward that subject, man, whose study seems to require no more than introspection and can be readily fragmented into sentiments, affections, habits, preconceptions, moralizing (as distinct from morality), and (in contemporary jargon) behavioristic patterns.

Following his early, aborted attempts at geometry, Hume opted instead to become the Copernicus of moral philosophy. All he achieved in that respect was a sustained plea for utilitarianism. It undoubtedly represented a radical turn, although in a direction which was the very opposite to the epistemological stance of Copernicus, who, to recall Galileo's famous words, chose to "commit a rape of his senses."[40] The utilitarianism of Humean ethics was a logical sequel to that dismemberment of man into a heap of sensations which is the hallmark of Hume's *Treatise on Human Nature.*[41] The inner logic leading to such an outcome has often been told, not always deplored, and hardly ever viewed against the hallowed shibboleth that Hume carried on in the spirit of Newton. That shibboleth is a patent absurdity. Newton's work is impossible to grasp on the assumption that the cause-effect relationship, which physics must assume as long as it is a study of physical reality, can only be the object of a study of the physicist's imagining such reality. Physics, be it of Newton or of Einstein, presupposes far more than a projection of our slowly-formed and still-forming habits into the study of matter. Also, Hume's own work is impossible to grasp on strictly Humean grounds. In no way Hume could persuade his readers that there was at least one world, the world represented by Hume writing to them, existing independently of their sensations of it.

At any rate, if the cause-effect relationship is the result of slowly established habits, their extension to the impact of new and very unexpected events, let alone novel reasonings, is in no way legitimate. Hume was not authorized on the basis of his philosophy to expect (although he obviously wrote his *Treatise* in the expectation) that the intellectual world would make a Copernican turn under the impact of his book. Even to speak of such an effect demands a style which is unjustifiable within the Humean perspective.[42] The impact in question is mental and therefore the question arises: Did Hume speak of mind, intellect, let alone of soul? He did on a few occasions but he invariably took flight from the reality denoted by these words. For one thing, he was frightened by hellfire and brimstone sermons about man's being predestined to eternal damnation, a vision which a mere mention of the soul evoked in him. For another, he also realized that an admission of the reality of mind as distinct from sensations would make a shambles of his philosophical system. He took the easy way out. It consisted in a self-oblivious abandonment to the realm of instincts as exhaustive of human nature. They were satisfied by his playing back-gammon, though not by his playing games with philosophy and reality.

With science no such game could be played. Hume therefore carefully avoided science, and certainly Newton's physics. The only time he spoke extensively of science, he made scientific genius crawl on its belly.[43] This should reveal something of the nature of the shibboleth about Hume as a Newtonian philosopher and also of Hume's philosophical work. Operating from Hume's conclusions, one cannot *do* science, as Einstein himself was to realize after his scientific creativity made him see the hollowness of Hume's dicta as well as of those of Mach, the late 19th-century counterpart of Hume. While this argument from Einstein's authority cannot be peremptory, a look at the standard which Hume provided for the evaluation of his work should seem to clinch the argument. That work, be it the *Treatise*, or the *Enquiry* or the *Essays* or the *Dialogues*, contains not a trickle of that science which is a combination of matters-of-fact and of mathematics. The absence of mathematics in Hume's books will not be disputed. As to the matters-of-fact, Hume held them to be, at best, mere sensations. If more objective than mere sensations, any and all matters-of-fact could ring the death-knell for Hume's philosophy. The verdict was spelled out by Hume himself. For if it was true that when running havoc over libraries all volumes void of matters-of-fact or mathematics were to be thrown into the flames,[45] how could any exception be taken to the books written by David Hume?

Some iconoclasm is also in order as one turns to the impact of Hume on Kant. Was Hume the essential prompting for Kant toward a more critical, deeper metaphysics and abstractive thinking? Undoubtedly, Kant was not willing to live on the ruins of an edifice, Wolffian idealism, which he saw collapsing as he read Hume. But a scepsis, such as the one exuding from Hume, could hardly prompt, let alone sustain, a labor which kept Kant in its grip for almost forty years. He was just entering his forties when he made his first jottings of a most laborious work, the *Critique of Pure Reason*, to be followed by other critiques, one on ethics, one on esthetics, one on religion, one on education, and last but not least, a vast manuscript of over two thousand folio pages. It is now known as the *Opus postumum*, but it should have been given the title, *The Critique of the Exact Sciences*.

Behind such a sustained labor there must have been some very special perspective. The foregoing reference to the exact sciences may indicate that the perspective was Newtonian science. Kant was very much taken by it without ever making a dent in the *Principia* or in any good book on physics which Euler, d'Alembert, the Bernoullis, and lesser figures had already made available in large quantities. Kant's illusion about being familiar with Newton was indeed the cause of his great misstep as a philosopher. In pondering in 1763 the clarity of principles in ethics and natural theology he recognized that philosophy must not have a foundation in a science outside it, such as geometry. This was a step in the right direction. In the next breath, Kant reversed his step by declaring that philosophy should be modeled on Newtonian physics, certainly a science outside philosophy.[46]

Kant's emancipation of man

A metaphysics as certain as Newtonian physics was not for Kant an aim in itself. As to his true aim Kant did not leave us in the dark. As a matter of fact, few other philosophers stated more clearly than Kant did, his principal aim. Kant did so at a time, 1765, when he definitely turned his back on everything he had written previously and kept all his energies for the task to be achieved: "If there is any science which man is really in need of, it is that which teaches him how to fulfill properly the position assigned to him in creation and from which he can learn what he must be in order to be a man."[47] This is not to suggest that previously Kant had not been concerned with man. His cosmogony, written in 1755, is full of passages in which man appears as the center and aim of at least the formation of the earth.[48] The course on logic, which Kant began to give shortly afterwards, also shows Kant's preoccupation with man. Its introduction contains a list of four short questions to which all philosophy can be reduced: "1. What can I know? 2. What ought I to do? 3. What may I hope? 4. What is man?"[49]

In neither work did Kant give an unambiguous and straightforward answer to that last question. Not that the cosmogony had not contained some indication as to the direction Kant ultimately was to take concerning man. Man is a creature there but not necessarily a created being. The material creation must, according to Kant, be necessarily supplemented by thinking natures suited to the condition of matter on each and every planet. Unlike others, such as Lambert and Herschel, Kant did not put living beings on comets and the sun. He could do much worse. Like Locke before him, Kant too courted the idea of thinking matter.[50] Kant avoided being outspoken on this subject, although Frederick the Great, to whom he dedicated his cosmogony, was an avowed materialist. He avoided offering a clear-cut answer to the question—what is man? —even in his favorite course, anthropology, which he gave over thirty years. The course was mostly descriptive, interspersed with anecdotes about customs and idiosyncrasies, but also contained some

philosophical parts and revealing comments, at times with no obvious connection to the subject matter discussed.

Kant's discourse, in the anthropology, on man's cognitive
powers, much of which could have been taken from Wolff's psychology, seemed to be leading up to an acceptance of the great
variety of thinking which nature produces in mankind. Nature,
Kant wrote, "puts on a show in the theatre of observers and
thinkers that is worth seeing for its infinite variety."[51] Kant's students could readily see this from the various anecdotes. They could
even understand that Kant held high an ideal of man who thought
for himself, who was able to enter into the mentality of others, and
who was consistent in all his thoughts. One wonders what they
thought on hearing Kant declare by way of grand conclusion: "The
most important revolution within man is 'his leaving the tutelage
for which he himself is responsible.' Before this revolution others
did his thinking for him, and he merely imitated them or let them
lead him by guide ropes. Now he risks walking forward with his
own feet on the ground of experience, even if he wobbles along."[52]

Kant was too much of an obedient civil servant to create the
impression that he had a political revolution in mind. He was never
to risk his professorial security by his ideas. As to the tutelage, it
was not the first time used by Kant in the context. He had already
referred to the tutelage of children under parents, of women under
their husbands, and of the laity under the clergy. Kant's students
knew of course that early in his career he had been in trouble with
prominent Pietist clergymen in Königsberg. Kant meant much
more than emancipation from clergy and church. He could have
made matters absolutely clear by stating that he spoke under the influence of Rousseau. Perhaps to mask himself before the public,
Kant made but rare and usually critical references to Rousseau even
in publications which stood in deep debt to Rousseau's writings.
While the name of Rousseau was not to be celebrated in Prussia, it
was held high in Kant's study, whose sole ornament was a print of
Rousseau's portrait. It could hardly pass unnoticed by Kant's close
friends admitted there. They knew that sometime in 1762 the
almost impossible happened. For days Kant broke his daily
schedule, a schedule so rigid that Kant's neighbors could regulate
their clocks by his daily walks. Kant's close friends found him deep-

ly agitated, quite changed from his usually composed self. The professor extraordinarius was clearly in the grip of something very extraordinary. Kant was reading the most extraordinary novel: Rousseau's *Julie, ou la Nouvelle Héloise* which had been first published a year before under the title, *Lettres des deux amans, habitans d'une petite ville au pied des Alpes.*

In *Julie* one certainly had an extraordinary portrayal of existence as being equivalent to ceaseless longing, an attitude which Rousseau saw embodied in women. Intellectual appraisal of reality had no room in a world view which prompted the most often quoted phrase in *Julie*: "In this world only the land of chimeras is worthy of dwelling."[53] It took a most "extraordinary" professor like Kant, who brushed women aside as merely having the "virtues of women,"[54] to see *Julie* as an unqualified blessing, and an intellectual one at that! Rousseau for him was not only a mind of unusual brilliance, but "a genius with a perception, the like of which no other age or people could boast."[55] In Kant's view Rousseau was the first to discover the true nature of man hidden beneath its greatly varying forms. Rousseau vindicated Providence in respect to the laws of human nature just as Newton's laws vindicated Providence in respect to nature at large.[56] If such was the case, Kant could but take Rousseau for a supreme guide, which is what happened. "Rousseau set me right," Kant wrote, and gave also the specific sense in which this was to be taken. Until then Kant felt that learning was an aim in itself and he looked at the uneducated as rabble. Henceforth he was to regard himself of less use than a mere laborer unless all his intellectual efforts could be seen useful for a single purpose: "to restore the rights of man."[57]

Restoration of the rights of man is attempted in various ways—some superficial, some profound. Kant, of course, attempted it in the most fundamental way conceivable, by trying to establish man in his own right as a fully autonomous being. He was cautious even in making notes. Only in retrospect can we see the significance of the phrase, already quoted, about the only science really needed by man. Only in retrospect can we see what he meant, as, in 1765, he jotted the phrase: "Metaphysics may be said to be a science about the limits of human reason."[58] His confidant, Marcus Herz, a physician and former student, whom Kant used as a sounding board in the years preceding the publication of the *Critique*, could hardly realize what Kant meant upon receiving word from him in 1773 that he was "soon to give philosophy a new turn, and one far more advantageous to religion and morality."[59] In hindsight the matter must be clear, and certainly the true nature of that "great light" which, so Kant reminisced, came to him in 1769. The light was, as Kant's notes testify,[60] the vista of an intellectual justification of the moral autonomy of man, responsible not to God, but only to himself.

As it happened, the light was a blinding glitter of arcane diction. Herz was the first to be tortured by it after Kant asked him to read the manuscript of the *Critique*. Having read half of it Herz gave it back to Kant, fearful that were he to read the whole he might go mad. The *Critique* was indeed a maddening work, but a Pascal would have been needed to put this across right there and then in an inimitable phrase. Pierre Duhem, who knew by heart Pascal's *Pensées*, found there the best means to lay bare the maddening character of the *Critique* in describing it as the "longest, most obscure, most confused, and most pedantic commentary" on Pascal's words about man's inability to prove, an inability insurmountable by any dogmatism.[61] Obscurity, length and pedantry were partly responsible for the assent of many to Kant's basic contention that critical reflection on knowledge could be the first step in philosophy. He and countless others failed to see that criticism presupposes knowledge itself. To emphasize such an error may seem to some a matter of pedantry. Yet it is the most colossal and portentous error one can commit in philosophy. Most colossal in proportion, because it leads to sheer subjectivism, nay solipsism, which cuts one off from the rest of the universe. Most portentous in consequence because on its basis man can believe he is his own master in the strictest and most fundamental sense.

Man as archangel

There is much more than meets the eye in Cassirer's comment that "what Kant prized in Rousseau was the fact that he had distinguished more clearly than others between the mask that man wears and his actual visage."[62] Rousseau claimed that man in his true nature was a noble savage. A professed intellectualist like Kant could not welcome an invitation to sentimentalist primitivism. While Rousseau despised culture, Kant was a worshipper of it. Kant's response to the outpouring of sentiment from every page of *Julie*, and even of *Emile*, was perhaps a more complex matter. Kant's avowed aversion to sentiment may have been a defense mechanism designed to mask a thorough subjectivism in his thinking, the deepest form of entrapment by sentiment. It should be no surprise that his work on aesthetics, the *Critique of Judgment*, in which Kant could indulge his sentiments without embarrassment, was to become Kant's best book. He struggled, he claimed, to remain free of Rousseau's sentimentalism so that he might see what lay beneath it.[63] He decided to intellectualize Rousseau's message, hardly a difficult task, since surely it was obvious all along that what Rousseau wanted was freedom from any transcendental constraint or dependence.

The rest is well known. The *Critique of Pure Reason* is a vast effort to establish on the so-called critical principle the claim that universe, soul, and God—the three main objects of metaphysics— were but the bastard products of the cravings of the human intellect. If such is the case, man can indeed be his own master, he can even create his own religion without becoming truly religious. Kant never went so far as to recognize a personal God as he tried, on the basis of practical reason, to rehabilitate God, soul, and universe. According to what may be Kant's most concise statement on the subject, "God is the moral-practical reason legislating for itself." Immediately preceding this phrase in the *Opus postumum* Kant makes it clear that such a God is man himself: "God is not a being outside me but merely a thought within me."[64]

That man was his own God, if he needed one, was evidently Kant's conclusion. For the most part Kant satisfied himself by describing man as essentially superior over all creatures on earth. A particularly telling statement of his in this connection is to be found in the opening paragraph of his anthropology. There man is described as infinitely superior, a qualification which may not necessarily have been intended in any vague sense: "The fact that man can have the idea 'I' raises him infinitely above all the other beings living on earth. By this he is a *person*; and by virtue of his unity of consciousness through all the changes he may undergo, he is one and the same person—that is, a being altogether different in rank and dignity from *things*, such as irrational animals, which we can dispose of as we please. This holds even if he cannot yet say 'I'; for he still has it in mind. So any language must *think* 'I' when it speaks in the first person, even if it has no special word to express it. For this power (the ability to think) is *understanding*." For all its merits, the passage is patently lop-sided. It represents man as if he were mere intellectuality. As one would expect, undue emphasis on the intellectual side of man would easily become a trap. Indeed, in the very next paragraph, in talking about the rise of consciousness in children, Kant presents it as a second phase of an evolution. The first phase is not the knowledge of things but the feeling of oneself: "Before, the child merely felt himself, now he thinks himself."[65]

From this vantage point the whole coming of Kantian epistemology can be foreseen. The merits of that epistemology, as codified in the *Critique*, have been the subject of many heated discussions—which will continue as long as one overlooks the fact that Kant meant it to be evaluated by its usefulness as a tool for inquiries into other fields, science included. On Kant's *Critique of Practical Reason* no time should be wasted. He had no right to write it. Whatever is valuable in his critique of aesthetics, or judgment, it does not require the *Critique of Pure Reason* as its justification. Kant's critique of religion leaves religion without God and without worshippers; certainly a fruitful outcome for atheists. (Significantly, in his critique of education, Kant stressed that children should be taught rather the negative than the positive in matters of religion.[66]) Those who consider all this a too-sweeping judgment on Kant will find little room for disagreeing in regard to the *Opus postumum*. It is Kant's legislation, on the basis of the first critique, on the exact sciences. The legislation is antiscience throughout, the kind of counterscience which first raised its head in Naturphilosophie.[67]

Naturphilosophie is antiscience because it is sheer subjectivism. Subjectivism of the weaker, superficial kind is founded on the sentiments. The real threat is posed by a subjectivism of the intellect. Such is the subjectivism of Kantian philosophy. Its springs are not in the sentiments but in the intellectual pride which was a distinctive feature of Kant's mental physiognomy. No one can be assumed to be without a strong touch of hubris who at the age of thirty, with no training in Newtonian physics, believed that he had said that very last word on the physics of cosmogony of which Newton despaired.[68] It was the same hubris that made Kant believe 25 years later that he had put metaphysics in its final form after millennia of futile efforts by a galaxy of geniuses. Kant's phrase, "I do not have the pride to become an archangel, my pride is merely that I am a man,"[69] may make one think that the man protesteth too much. Lucifer did not believe himself to *be* God: he merely declined to serve; a proud archangel he was. Kant could do much worse. He spoke of man as "that being" which *was* God. He did so in the *Opus postumum* in a sequence of phrases too orderly to be ascribed either to haste or to decrepitude.[70]

With a mere man the wish to become an archangel, let alone God, would have been a sign of insanity. For the same man to think that he knew things in a way subtly matching the powers of an archangel was a possibility still on this side of derangement. But a sin it was! Kant's punishment was subtle. He was allowed to range far and wide. He was free to think that he knew not only the structure of thought but also everything on earth. He indeed discoursed from his armchair in Königsberg of far away lands and peoples as if he had been better informed than were world travelers. He could think that he was able to fathom the purpose of nature as providing everywhere on the globe for the spreading of mankind. He was, however, not allowed to see that he merely trapped himself in naiveté and contradiction as he made declarations such as this in his *Eternal Peace*: "The maternal providence of nature is most wonderfully manifested by the singular manner in which she furnishes . . . those countries destitute of vegetation with wood without which the inhabitants could have neither canoes, weapons, or huts."[71] Kant seemed indeed to see himself as the angel bringing the good tidings of peace to all men, not so much to men of God's good will, as to men free of God's tutelage.

The same context also shows a Kant who, like Descartes, tries to hide behind a mask. And yet the posture of an angel is all too visible there. A flying figure, whose crash into the seas had by then been a very old story, appears in the same phrase in which Kant covered up his dismissal of Providence with a specious reference to

Nature. The word 'providence', he wrote, "intimates a pretended knowledge of its mysteries, and a flight as temerarious as that of Icarus, towards the sanctuary of its impenetrable designs." Kant was merely another Icarus. For his temerity he had one penalty. The very same *Critique* which established man's autonomy by barring God from man's reach, barred man from ever reaching to the universe and to its science. As the sundry dicta of Fichte, Schelling, Hegel and of all the Hegelian right and left, proved, the man emancipated by the *Critique* could only play the role of such an angel whose wings had to melt on being exposed to real light.

Hegel's man as World-Spirit

Such a penalty, consisting in a disqualification from science, ought not to appear too light in an age of science. There was a further, far more universal and devastating penalty implied in the logic of taking man for mind, pure and autonomous A generation after Kant found his liberation in Rousseau, the same happened to Hegel as well. The immediate effect was the end of Hegel's pursuit of theology and Lutheran ministry in the Tübingen Seminary.[72] Being no less an intellectualist (and thwarted sentimentalist) than Kant, Hegel, too, went on to intellectualize Rousseau. Of course, he could hardly avoid working along a pattern already set by Fichte and Schelling. Roads for originality appeared to them to have been left open only in the direction set by Kant. The most promising line of advance seemed to point toward the keystone joining the two arches of the Kantian theory of knowledge. Fichte and Schelling could plausibly argue that the imagination, through which Kant tried to connect the arches of sensations and categories, was not genuinely intellectual. Hegel too was right in claiming that will and beauty, which Fichte and Schelling respectively proposed as keystones, meant no less an abandonment of pure intellectuality. Hegel proposed mind itself for that role. As befitted a consistent systematizer, he proceded to the radical intellectualization of all. Man was certainly engulfed in it.

The claim that man was mind could not have been stated more clearly by Hegel. The circumstances, on at least one occasion, were just as telling as his declaration. Already forty-six, and except for a year or so in the University of Jena as assistant professor, reduced to private tutoring and to heading a gymnasium, Hegel felt, on delivering his inaugural lecture at the University of Heidelberg (1816) that his hour had come at last. Once more the finest truth and the worst error became dangerously juxtaposed. No Christian mindful of St. Augustine's warning, *intellectum valde ama,* could take exception to Hegel's declaration that "man cannot esteem too greatly the stature and power of his mind." But there was much more reason for concern than for cheer as Hegel added that "the courage of truth, a faith in the power of the mind, is the prime requirement of philosophy and that man, being mind, may and should consider himself worthy of the Highest."[73]

Hegel's description of man as "mind" was not a matter of exalted rhetoric. It was the keystone of his philosophy and message. Man as mind was also the World-Spirit. Man as body had therefore to share the fate of the World-Spirit, of which physical Nature was not a creation but an alienation. The aim of philosophy, as Hegel saw it, was the liberation of mind from its bondage to body so that the World-Spirit too might be liberated from its imprisonment in Nature. Hegel felt that as far as the World-Spirit was concerned, the prospects were especially good. With Napoleon sequestered on St. Helena, "the torrent of reality has been stopped" and the World-Spirit, too busy until then with external reality (the din of Napoleonic wars), could now "turn inward and concentrate." Being mind, man therefore had to fall in step with the dialectic of the World-Spirit in the certainty that full inwardness would obtain for him full grasp and control of Nature, that is, externality: "The initially closed and concealed essence of the universe has no power that can resist the courage of cognition; the essence of the universe must disclose itself to him, revealing its riches and its depths and giving them up to him for his enjoyment."[74]

That for Hegel man was mind had already been clear to readers of his *Phenomenology of Mind,* published in 1807. They were soon to read Hegel's detailed account of the conquest of Nature through the interiorization of the mind. Hegel arrived in Heidelberg with a fairly complete manuscript of his *Encyclopedia of the Sciences,* which saw print as he finished his first year in that city.[75] He was not yet halfway through his second year when he was eagerly invited by authorities in Berlin to take the chair of philosophy there. It tells something of those times that instead of putting an end to Hegel's academic career, the *Encyclopedia* rather helped to catapult its author to the highest position to which a German academic could then aspire. In 1818 Naturphilosophie reigned supreme and its dévotés wanted not only the control of the philosophical faculties but also of the faculties of science. Some German scientists despaired indeed of their very future.[76] Hegel himself pressed the cause of Naturphilosophie relentlessly. Between 1817 and 1831, the year of his death, he brought out his *Encyclopedia,* the quintessence of the obscurantism of Naturphilosophie, in three editions, each considerably larger than the last.[77] Possibly he sensed that the ultimate unmasking of Idealism would come from the hands of science. To forestall this outcome science had to be turned into Naturphilosophie. Scientists and science were, however, much harder to crack than imagined by Hegel and Hegelians. In fact, as it turned out, even some scientists, imbued with Idealism, were weened from it simply by facing up to what they were doing as scientists.

Most German scientists were from the start deeply resentful of Naturphilosophie and especially of some Naturphilosophes. A glance at the table of contents of the *Encyclopedia* was often enough to make a scientist suspicious of it. To verify his suspicions he had only to read the paragraph in which Hegel summarized the message of the *Encyclopedia.* There he painted in quick strokes the deployment of the Idea through gravity into the "free heavenly bodies," in which it achieved the first stage of its "externality." The latter then shaped itself into "individual unities" through physical movement and chemical processes. Organic life arose when gravity was released "into members possessing subjective unity." Thus was the stage set for the grand conclusion: "The aim of these lectures is to convey an image of nature, in order to subdue this Proteus: to find in this externality only the mirror of ourselves, to see in nature a free reflection of spirit: to understand God, not in the contemplation of spirit, but in this His immediate existence."[78]

Whatever the reaction of a practicing scientist to the sheer pantheism of this passage and to its rank subjectivism and apriorism, he must have realized that it cannot be germane to an experimentation aimed at fathoming, in a laborious way, some of Nature's secrets. The interiorized mind knows, if Hegel is right, through reflecting on its own dialectic, what Nature is like. Nature as seen through the lenses of Hegelian dialectic is a far cry from the Nature science pre-supposes. To be sure, Hegel was shrewd enough to make it appear that his dialectic would lead, say, to the elliptical orbit of planets and to the inverse square law of gravitation. In all appearance, he could not care less whether his dicta on space, time, matter, gravity, stars, planets, falling bodies, electricity, and chemical reactions would ring a bell with physicists and chemists. Chinese would have sounded more familiar to most German physicists around 1817 and later than did the declaration on the very first page of the *Encyclopedia* that "space was the immediated indifference of nature."[79]

Subsequent pages of the *Encyclopedia* were distinguished by similar utterances. Time was the negativity of space, provided space "posited itself in such a way as to remain indifferent to its immobile collaterality."[80] That mathematical physics was not to be mastered easily could be suspected from Hegel's remark that quantity represented externality at its extreme.[81] True enough, few Hegelians ever achieved outstanding competence in higher mathematics and in mathematical physics. The Hegelian definition of matter as "the immediately identical and existent unity of place and motion"[82] must have appeared no less arcane than the definition of attraction, strictly distinct from gravity, as "the general sublation of juxtaposition."[83] Hegel achieved an unusual degree of stylistic clarity as he declared matter to be "spatial separation,"[84] but he hardly made life thereby much easier for physicists. These could only gasp on hearing Hegel declare that the pendulum was brought to rest by gravity and not by friction.[85] They were also told that Newton's building on Kepler's work shows "how reflection which fails to get to the bottom of things can distort and pervert the truth."[86]

Newton was, of course, excoriated for his theory of colors, a point which certainly earned for Hegel praises from Goethe,[87] who, it is well to recall, reached Hegelian heights of self-delusion with his claim, which he maintained to the end of his life, that as a poet he was inferior to what he was as a physicist![88] Hegel's dicta on the starry realm were predicated on his contrasting light with matter. The former was "pure self," the latter, "the equivalent lack of self," was "darkness."[89] Later Hegel declared: "the sky is night, it is black,"[90] by which he meant blackness itself. The axial rotation of planets was for him an expression of animation.[91] No wonder. If a proof were needed on the identity of Hegelian physics with Aristotelian physics, in which the living organism was the chief explanatory device and also the main barrier to progress, it could be found on the half-dozen pages which Hegel devoted to the "elements." They were none other than earth, water, air, and fire![92] He held them high against the so-called chemical elements which he could not, of course, entirely dismiss half a century after Lavoisier. In fact he turned them inside out. A case in point is his definition of hydrogen as "the positive side of determinateness in opposition, or differentiated nitrogen."[93] The organismic viewpoint unabashedly called for its logical sequence, anthropomorphism, when Hegel broached the topic of electricity. For him electrical tension was the "intrinsic selfhood of the physical totality of a body which maintains itself in its contact with another body." Through electrical tension the "body's youthfulness breaks out; it raises itself on its hind legs." Electrical phenomena were for Hegel "an upsurge of anger in the body."[94] All this could perhaps qualify as poetry in prose, but two centuries after Galileo hardly appear as progress in science.

No book by a systematic mind would fail to contain a passage or two whose full meaning can only be seen in the light of one or several of his other works. Hegel's concluding remarks in the introductory chapter of the history of earth in the *Encyclopedia* are an illustration. North and South America were dismissed by him as a mere "buttment of the Old World," which in turn was seen by him in its three parts as the embodiment of the unfolding of the World-Spirit. Africa, the primary part of the Old World, hardly fared well in that dialectic. Hegel ascribed the scorching heat enveloping much of that continent to its being "equivalent to the compact metal or the lunar principle." For Africa this meant, in the Hegelian perspective, that "its humanity is sunk in torpor, that Africa is the dull spirit which does not enter into consciousness." Asians would hardly be pleased by Hegel's description of their continent as "the bacchantic eccentricity of the comet, the wild middle, which brings forth only from itself, engenders without form and is unable to master its centre." As to Europeans, they could only be concerned.

While Europe was defined as the "rational region of the Earth, or consciousness," Germany was made its very center.[95]

Angels playing beasts

The rest can be told in a few words. That for Hegel history and society held no secret will not surprise those who remember the Introduction to his *Logic* where he described that subject, recast by him, as "the realm where truth appears without veil exactly as it is." It took the wit of at least an angel to imagine that such a logic was "the presentation of God as He existed in His eternal being before the creation of nature and of finite intellects."[96] What Hegel held of state, military caste, and war are too well known to be repeated here.[97] He must be given credit for being so consistent as to declare that world history, being an unfolding of the Spirit, "is not a theater of happiness. Periods of happiness are blank pages in it."[98] The hundred-and-fifty years after Hegel, especially the last fifty, have cruelly illuminated the true impact of Hegel's opinions.[99] The whole outcome could also be foreseen. A few years after Hegel's death, Heine warned the French not to take German Idealism lightly. One of the only two errors in those prophetic pages of Heine's *Germany* concerns his advice to the French, although it was but half an error. While he warned the French against disarmament, he urged them not to intervene militarily on seeing the logic of Idealism complete its full circle beyond the Rhine. Heine, who saw that Hegel had completed what Kant started, expected (this was the other error) the final dénouement in his lifetime. Apart from that, he could appear clairvoyance itself. He conjured up Kantians "with sword and axe," who "will mercilessly rummage around in the soil of our European culture in order to eradicate the last roots of the past." He also foresaw the outcome when the Cross, "that restraining talisman," would be broken to pieces. Yet Heine was not a clairvoyant, let alone a prophet. After all, he himself noted in the same context that "thought precedes the deed as lightning precedes thunder." Again, no clairvoyance was needed to see that Kant's efforts to undermine the proofs of the existence of God pervaded all his works. And so did his effort to turn man into a fully autonomous being, or superman, the modern version of angels of old. Modern times have given indeed apocalyptic proof of the beastly behavior of man turned "angel" in telling witness to the Great Beast of the Apocalypse, the prototype of all fallen angels.

II

GLORIFIED APE

"Those who despise men, and put them on a level with the brutes, yet wish to be admired and believed by men, . . . contradict themselves by their own feelings."
—Pascal, Pensées No. 404

Rousseau's saintly simians

If there is a difference it must be between one who hides under a mask and another who does his utmost to lay himself bare. The usually withdrawn Descartes and the irrepressibly communicative Rousseau were indeed very different. Descartes' mind was riveted on science, which was foreign to Rousseau's thinking. Descartes was an all too ready source of ideas, whereas Rousseau confessed that ideas took shape in his head "with the most incredible difficulty."[1] Descartes staked everything on mathematical intellectuality. The only passions he could discourse upon were those of the mind. There was nothing poetical in his writings. As if by irony, it was a namesake of Rousseau, Jean-Baptiste, who reported, three years after Jean Jacques' birth, a favorite saying of the poet and literary critic, Boileau: "The philosophy of Descartes cut poetry at its throat."[2] As for Rousseau himself, he was the poet of prose form, if ever there was one. Yet for all their differences, Descartes and Rousseau played, with or without a mask, much the same role. Both were catalysts of the two main modern trends whose chief feature is to take only one half of human nature. Descartes seized on the mind and boosted man into an angel. Rousseau took the sentiments, but having no eyes for the head, he aimed at the heart and hit the target somewhat lower, where the beast loves to reside in man.[3]

Had Rousseau been but a persuasive profligate, he would not be specially remembered today. Rousseau is special, because, though a scoundrel, he wanted to be remembered as a saint. He threw his *Confessions* as a challenge at anyone who, after reading it, dared to say: "I was a better man than he."[4] To the less insightful, from queen to commoner, the author of *Confessions*, of *Julie*, and of *Emile* was indeed a saint. Marie Antoinette traveled as a pilgrim, as did thousands of others, the fifty miles from Paris to Ermenonville, where Jean Jacques lay buried under poplar trees on a small island. In their ardor several Englishmen swam across the river when the ferry failed to show up. If the pilgrim were a priest, a liturgy might be improvised. Accompanied by a baron, "who felt purer" by touching Rousseau's snuff-box, the abbé Brizard felt his own trembling to be similar to that of the priestess approaching Apollo's sanctuary. The abbé chanted passages from Rousseau's writings as if they were Holy Writ, offered a sacrifice by burning pages of a pamphlet that attacked Rousseau, gave an alms of six gold coins to a poor woman standing by, and eulogized the "shoes of the man who never walked but in the path of virtue." It was in order to become "imbued with virtue that I went there," reminisced the abbé, obviously unsure of his calling.[5]

In speaking of virtue in general and of the virtues of Rousseau in particular, the baron and the priest knew, of course, what they meant. Their idol recognized only a virtue void of the sense of duty. Could virtue, Rousseau himself asked, "which is effort and struggle, rule in the midst of softness and sweet delights?" The answer was an identification of the virtuous and of the natural, coupled with a defiant dismissal of the notion of duty inasmuch as it implied self-denial. Man (Rousseau was speaking of himself as well) "would be good because nature made him such. He would do good because he would find it sweet to do it. But if it were a question of fighting his most cherished desires and of tearing apart his heart in order to fulfill his duty, would he do that too? I doubt it. The law of nature, or at least her voice, does not go that far. In that case another voice would be needed and nature would have to fall silent."[6] Rousseau believed he would "blaspheme," were he to burden such a nature with original sin.[7] When he merely stated that "the yoke of nature was easy,"[8] he still sounded blasphemous enough for Christian ears.

A nature free of moral commandments, implied in the notion of duty, was a nature existing for itself. The "other voice" was inadmissible because it bespoke nature's dependence on a Creator who revealed Himself through nature, through one's conscience, and through a special series of acts as well. Not surprisingly, Rousseau was not concerned with nature at large. The universe, which he called "a woman's book,"[9] existed for him only as a prompting of sentiments. "To exist is to feel,"[10] was Rousseau's version of the self-centeredness of Descartes' *cogito ergo sum*. Nor was that uncreated nature, postulated by Rousseau, as wide as the entire realm of sentiments including the voice of conscience. That nature irresistibly shrank to one's amorous impulses. Nature in that sense could not remain in the long run an unqualified bliss. As Rousseau himself came to realize, bliss turned into an abyss "for the poor luckless mortal" he was. But there, at the very bottom of that abyss, he felt his ultimate satisfaction. It consisted in his deliverance from depending for enjoyment on anything external to himself. There one "savors nothing except oneself and one's own existence and as long as that condition lasts, one is enough for oneself as God is [for Himself]." Indeed there everything was as "impassible as God Himself."[11]

The saying, "You must be yourself," which Rousseau liked to repeat in his last years,[12] should therefore seem to be a far cry from Socrates' "know thyself." With Socrates, a teacher of Plato, ideas and norms bore witness to a transcendent order, from which he derived such a firm conviction about the immortality of the soul as to drink the hemlock, although escape from prison was within his easy reach. With Rousseau immanence reigned supreme. Any reasoning that pointed beyond nature invited his stricture. He felt it to be his chief task to save the youth from ensnarement by metaphysics. Emile was told that "the jargon of metaphysics has never led to the discovery of a single truth, and has filled philosophy with absurdities of which we are ashamed as soon as we strip them of their long words."[14] Sophie, Emile's counterpart, received similar warning: "In philosophy substance, soul, body, eternity, movement, liberty, necessity, contingency, etc., are so many words which one is forced to use every moment and no one has ever understood." Untrained in the sciences, such a young woman could hard-

ly suspect the true nature of that warning which also included a
debunking of the simplest form of physics and of Newton himself
for his not having doubted the finer points of electricity.[15] Society as
a whole was warned against the reasoned vistas of transcendence
when Rousseau characterized abstractions as so many "unnatural
operations" that turn man into a corrupted animal.[16]

Yet even in that latter respect there would still be some sym-
pathy for Rousseau. One could list endlessly books and articles,
learned and popular, written during the last hundred years, or even
during the last few decades, which would contain statements similar
to the one in Rousseau's famed *Discourse on the Origin of Inequality*: "Every animal has ideas, since it has sense; it even com-
bines those ideas in a certain degree; and it is only in degree that
man differs, in this respect, from the brute."[17] Authors of the same
books would not, however, sympathize with Rousseau's desperate
effort to save free will for man.[18] They would simply state that what
Rousseau held to be valid of the savage (ape), was strictly true of
man as well: "The only gods he recognizes in the universe are food,
a female, and sleep; the only evils he fears are pain and hunger."[19]
Again, those authors would not join Voltaire's protest, who wrote
to Rousseau after receiving a copy of the *Discourse*: "No one has
ever displayed so much wit as you did in trying to turn us into
brutes; to read your book makes one long to go on all fours. As,
however, it is now more than sixty years since I lost that habit, I
feel that unfortunately it is impossible for me to resume it. I leave
that natural pattern for those who are more worthy of it than you
and I."[20] The two centuries that have gone by since Rousseau have
been enough to carry his glorification of the ape to its logical conclusion, which is the glorification of the rat and of animals even
lower yet. The development was inevitable once Rousseau had been
accepted as "the new god of sensations."[21] The latest phase of that
trend is no longer the ratomorphic view of man held by behaviorists
of a now bygone generation. The advance from rats to ants, the
models of human behavior in sociobiology, has not, however,
changed the principle of research described half a century ago as the
resolve "not to attribute to humans any characteristic that cannot
be demonstrated in lower animals."[22]

Rousseau would certainly have made a somewhat similar statement had he been capable of a modest measure of abstraction. The view of man, as articulated by him, would be difficult to evaluate scientifically. Radical sentimentalism, a kind of *l' art pour l'art*, is not a subject matter for science. But since that view took the Western World by storm, and under different labels still holds it in its grip, men of science could not escape its influence. The study of the history and philosophy of science years ago outgrew that infantile stage in which the thinking of men of science was portrayed as sheer objectivity. Indeed that same study has in recent years produced startling evidence of the vast influence which a view of man, such as Rousseau's, could have on scientific thought. That view certainly inspired some memorable scientific crudities. For example, the definition of man as a digestive tube, which secured notoriety for Cabanis. He argued, a few years before Rousseau's century was out, that the brain produced ideas in the same way in which, "the stomach and the bowels are destined to produce digestion, the liver to filter the bile, the parotids and the maxillary and sublingual glands to produce the salivary juices."[23] A key to his thought is not far to seek, for in his magnum opus on the relation of the physical and the moral, Cabanis observed that every philosopher formulates his idea of man, and that, among philosophers, Rousseau was the greatest.[24] The scientific crudities offered by Cabanis and Feuerbach, for another example, who stated that "man is what he eats,"[25] deserve no rebuttal. When articulated in a sophisticated way, Rousseau's view of man still produces unexpected rebuttals even within the circle of its dévotés. About the phrase, "under precisely controlled conditions an animal does as it damn well pleases," which graces the walls of more than one prominent animal behavioral laboratory, [26] those working there seem to know deep in their hearts that it is more than a boastful mockery. Rousseau would have found much solace in that phrase, devastating as it may appear for his view that, of all animals, man alone is free. For the phrase is an endorsement of the supreme tenet of Rousseau's creed: pleasures, of animals or of men, will ultimately prevail over any controlling force, be it religion, philosophy, or even science.

Science manhandled

Science could only be a supreme threat to man, whom Rousseau defined as the god of his sensations, pleasures, and satisfactions. The laws established by science are serenely unmindful of pleasure or pain, good or evil. Nor does science provide guidelines to assure the beneficial use of the magnificent and powerful tools it creates. No Newton was needed to perceive this. Some time before Newton became a world celebrity, there arose animated discussions, in France as well as in England, between humanists and scientists.[27] Although all too often the quarrel between "ancients and moderns"[28] degenerated into an unabashed struggle for positions of influence, the quarrel revealed enough awareness of deeper issues. In the 18th century the same problem, in the form of mechanism versus teleology, became a hotly-debated topic. The Académie des Sciences of Dijon gave no proof of originality when, in 1749, it offered a prize for the best essay on the subject: "Has the restoration of the arts and science had a purifying effect upon morals?"

Rousseau learned of the competition in October 1749, during one of his daily walks of a good five miles, from Paris to Vincennes, to cheer up Diderot who was in jail there. To make the journey less burdensome, he read as he walked. One day he took along the latest issue of the *Mercure de France* which carried a report on the prize offered by the Académie of Dijon. "The moment I read this I beheld another universe and became another man," Rousseau wrote many years later. Diderot hoped that Rousseau, who reached him "in a state of agitation bordering on delirium," would compete for the prize. "I did so," Rousseau reminisced, "and from that moment I was lost. All the rest of my life and of my misfortunes followed inevitably as a result of that moment's madness."[29]

A madness it was but not in the superficial sense in which Rousseau used that word. He was neither the first nor the last to call madness a course of action which puts one at loggerheads with many of one's contemporaries. Rousseau earned not only accolades but also many jeers for devoting the rest of his life, another thirty years, to describing, over thousands of captivating pages, that new universe he caught sight of during that fateful walk from Paris to Vincennes. The new sight itself was madness although it has in the long run been taken for a stroke of genius. Today, it forms the basic dogma of much of academic sophistication. The essence of that stroke is a transposition.[30] The perspective of good versus evil, of transcendental versus immanent, of absolute versus relative, of un-created versus created, of spiritual versus material, of natural versus supernatural, is transposed into the category of a mere pattern. The pattern is the contrast between primitive or natural versus cultured or unnatural. Rousseau's near-delirium was induced by the ease and apparent validity of the transposition. It seemed to eliminate in a single, non-metaphysical (and therefore easy) stroke all metaphysics, with its grave question marks. Rousseau could now abandon himself without restraint to his own nature, while inviting others to follow suit. He could engage in reasoning so simplistic as to be within the reach of almost anybody who had mastered the alphabet. In his pleasantly flowing phrases everybody could recognize himself in the grip of problems which, though in fact highly metaphysical, were described with the disarming simplicity of a born novelist as being merely matters of nature, if not merely matters of taste.

The arrestingly simple style and candid intimacy were only a part of Rousseau's strategy. It also included a debunking of learning as a possible harbinger and ally of metaphysics. Hence Rousseau's invectives against abstraction and reflection, hence his presentation of men and animals as identical beings as far as thinking goes. Rousseau's frequent recourse to monkeys in illustration of this or that point is no accident. He certainly glorified the ape. In an age like ours which takes metaphysics for a long-defunct species, it would be useless to argue that disaster looms large behind Rousseau's dismissal of mind and metaphysics. This age of ours, so proud of science, would perhaps see something of that disaster if exposed to the fate of learning and science within the perspective of the transposition which Rousseau found so liberating. The transposition simply makes science impossible. The impossibility is intimated even in Rousseau's characterization of his own prize-winning essay: "The work, though full of strength and fervour, is completely lacking in logic and order. Of all those that have proceeded from my pen it is the most feebly argued, the most deficient in proportion and harmony."[31]

These debilitating defects derived largely from the subject of the essay—science, a field always uncongenial for Rousseau. The "strength and fervour" in which he saw the merits of the essay were no less indicative of his frame of mind. His was a world-view in which irresistible currents of sentiments kept dissolving all contours of stability, order, and logic. Such a view is the opposite of that which science presupposes. Science cannot operate within a perspective which shows everything in the universe to be in flux and change. Rousseau preferred, even insisted upon such a universe: "All on earth is a continual flux which does not allow anything to take on a constant form."[32] A universe in flux is constantly dreamed about by those who recognize only the ever-shifting world of their moods and feelings. Glaring examples are the radical Romantics, old and new, almost invariably poets. "The wish—which ages have not yet subdued in man—to have no master save his mood," celebrated by Byron,[33] has also been the favorite theme of philosophers who characteristically choose novels as vehicles for their message. It was not without its significance that Sartre received the Nobel Prize in literature. Subtly poetical are also those who think that a world-view steeped in moods can be dressed in scientific terms. They make up the larger and far more vocal part of authors who, during the last two centuries, presented science to the common man. When they justify man's failure to live up to the dictates of objective norms, by claiming that heredity cannot be resisted, they simply urge man to yield to his moods, presumably until genetic engineering leaves in man only urges that need not be resisted. Such is also a "scientific" way of doing the transposition from ontological and metaphysical order to the realm of mere patterns. That patterns of behavior are today not only shifting but are most deliberately shifted brings the process full circle. The latter part of the process has only one redeeming value, the misguided honesty with which it is implemented. Here too Rousseau is in the lead.

The very recent explosion of openness, if it can be called honesty at all, with which public respectability is demanded for forms of behavior previously considered as grievously sinful or aberrant, is a mirror image of Rousseau's flaunting his sins as virtues in the *Confessions* and of his attack on science in the name of his ignorance of it, an ignorance amply revealed in his prize-winning essay. From the very start Rousseau openly admitted that he was to belittle science, which often meant for him all learning, including letters and history. Against the conflicting artificialities of the day he held high the honest man who "is an athlete, who loves to wrestle stark naked."[34] He clearly had in mind the noble savage and portrayed himself in that role. In laying the blame for the downfall of virtue at the door of the arts and sciences, the fruits of a recent intellectual "revolution" as he put it,[35] Rousseau could not have been more sweeping. He attributed the moral decay of ancient Egypt, Greece, Rome, and Byzantium to the spread of learning. He had a broadside for China, the illusory envy of Europe. Did their many learned men, Rousseau asked, save the Chinese from falling prey to all conceivable forms of vice, and from being dominated by ignorant Tartars?[36] Only those people remained virtuous, Rousseau insisted, that kept themselves free of learning, and he listed the Spartans, Persians, and the Germans of old. Rousseau took his Tacitus too seriously. He found witness on behalf of his thesis in Socrates and in the elder Cato as he piled one emotional phrase upon another.

After galloping over history, Rousseau made his reader believe that he was to turn to an analysis of science itself as the source of corruption. He merely offered claims, so many evidences of his method which consisted in erecting mountains of fallacy on grains of truth. He presented the sciences as born out of vice and having evil for their object. All the practice of the sciences was for him but a road full of deadly traps. He laid on the sciences the sole responsibility for the cacophony of opinions that prevailed. While certainly there were some physicists who "boldly explain the inexplicable mysteries of electricity, which will perhaps be forever the despair of real philosophers," Rousseau simply played to the galleries when he implied that "in all Europe" there was not "one single physicist" innocent on that score.[37] Rousseau held that all those exposed to the sciences "smile contemptuously at such old names as patriotism and religion."[38] He saw in the invention of printing only a means of spreading error and a breeding place, as he put it, "to the herd of text-book authors."[39] He particularly disliked the latter for throwing open to all the Temple of Learning. Great scientists—Rousseau claimed and seized once more on a grain of truth—were able to teach themselves.[40]

Of science proper Rousseau gave little if any specific. How could he? As he himself told in the *Confessions,* his only exposure to the sciences lasted but a few months, during the winter of 1737–38. He was already twenty-six, a bit late even for a genius to begin science. While he enjoyed a few popularizations of science, Euclid was not to his liking. The little astronomy he taught himself was purely descriptive.[41] No wonder that years later Rousseau reserved but a very minor role for the sciences in the education of youth. If *Emile* was to prove anything it was the disaster that resulted from a scientific education in which youngsters are expected to discover for themselves the basic rules of arithmetic.[42] Through *Emile* a new generation, hostile to the sciences, was to be raised. Rousseau himself took the lead. When not trying to obtain a favor, a prize, from learned societies, he lashed out at them with no restraint whatever. "Everyone knows," he wanted the younger generation exemplified in *Emile* to know, that "the learned societies of Europe are mere schools of falsehood and there are assuredly more mistaken notions in the Academy of Sciences in Paris than in a whole tribe of American Indians."[43] It was this man, almost entirely ignorant of and furiously hostile to the sciences, who set for the science of man a new course. He did so by fastening European thought to a new outlook on man. Man was henceforth autonomous, subject only to the voice of his sentiments and longings. He was a glorified ape who instinctively turned to the vistas of his simian ancestors. To view his mental faculties—imaginative creativity, moral sense, and last but not least his science—as evidences of something imperishable, and in a sense supernatural because given to him in a special creation, soon became an effrontery to scientific thought.

Had the French Revolution not unveiled something of the savagery of the noble savage, the first half of the nineteenth century would not have been an epoch in which even suggestions about the descent of man's body from animal origins were off limits. The Revolution owed much to Rousseau. Without giving credit to Rousseau, Diderot echoed him as he asked: "Do you wish to know the capsule story of almost all our misery? There once existed a natural man; there has been introduced within this man an artificial man and there has arisen in the cave a civil war which lasts throughout life."[44] The Revolution meant to put an end once and for all to that war within man, and was therefore above all an ideology which the Holy Alliance intended to repress as much as it opposed political stirrings. Although no part of the Alliance, England applauded first Burke's dictum that "man is by his constitution a religious animal,"[45] a capsule formula of the ideology sacred to the Alliance. Imposition of a particular ideology fosters all too effectively its opposite. France turned militantly Republican just as quickly as England put Christianity behind herself. Darwin was to marvel how things changed within one decade, the 1860s, separating the publication of the *Origin of Species* from the publication of the *Descent of Man.*[46] The *Origin* created a storm, whereas hardly a ripple was produced by the *Descent,* although it was unabashedly materialistic where it counted most, the question of man's origin and nature.

Darwin in the cause of apes

Long before the *Origin* Darwin was a materialist. He was in fact more of a dedicated materialist than a mere agnostic who by the logic of unstable equilibrium is toppled into materialism. The process is all too frequent and obvious. Lenin's description of agnosticism as "a fig leaf for materialism" merely expressed an elementary truth with no touch of originality.[47] To ignore that logic is to land in equivocations which pre-empt of its purpose even the most diligent scholarly research. Was it indeed possible for Darwin to reject from the start Christianity and remain open to theism to the end? The affirmative answer, as given recently,[48] depends on a studied ambivalence toward what is implied in theism. A god, whom Darwin's science forbids to be seen as a Creator, let alone a Person, is certainly different from the Christian God, but can still be called a God only in virtue of that twisted logic which the turning of man into a glorified ape inspires. In that logic, the notion of matter which thinks is respectable, the distinction between matter and mind is not. At any rate, no distinctions, consistently adhered to, are compatible with a logic which is inherited from Rousseau's romanticism. In Darwin's case his ineptness in matters of logic was certainly reinforced by his materialistic view of man to which he emphatically subscribed soon after his return from his voyage on The Beagle.

Darwin's early notebooks[49] amply testify to that crude materialism. Its debilitating impact on Darwin's discourses on the mind-body relationship was never considered by Darwin's admirers, and very rarely even by his best critics. Yet, that crude materialism is the clue to the somewhat muted materialism of Darwin's published writings. Like most other materialists, Darwin was disposed from the start to take thought as well as freedom lightly. Little allowance can be made for lack of precision and articulation in brief jottings when many of them are used in later publications.[50] Darwin's carefree equating of thought with sensory images[51] should leave one just as breathless as his seeing in the frolicking of his puppy a display of free will which he then quickly attributed to oysters, polyps, and to all animals.[52] His unusually primitive notion of science betrayed itself repeatedly in his choice and handling of illustrations. For example, in one instance he dwelt upon the ability of animals to balance themselves; in another, he asserted that the donkey "knows that one side of a triangle is shorter than two." It was in the same primitive vein that Darwin asked: "Why is thought, being a secretion of brain, more wonderful than gravity, a property of matter?"[54] All he saw behind this question was human arrogance. One could not expect Darwin to realize that gravity was an empty word—even most physicists failed to suspect this in the 1840s. He gave, however, not a fleeting thought to the fact that only brains capable of thinking could attribute gravity to matter, or to think of matter at all. He was no longer alive when better physicists replaced gravity with something more recondite and reliable, and began to marvel at the power of the mind.

This is not to suggest that Darwin failed to suspect the sheer magnitude of the task he faced in his effort to conquer mind by materialism. He knew that the human mind was, as he put it, "the citadel" which evolutionary thought had to conquer to be truly victorious.[55] More telling seems his admission in the same breath that "the problem of mind cannot be solved by attacking the citadel itself." Evidently it did not occur to him that by saying this he admitted defeat—a defeat all the more glaring because the "stable foundation" he sought for his arguments against the mind he never produced. Instead, he offered the quicksand of verbalizations embroidered with graphic observations which proved everything except the very point. To infer from this that Darwin was consciously cunning would be too daring a judgment were it not for Darwin's admission that he pursued a policy of dissimulation. In the same notebooks he set for himself the rule to avoid stating how far he believed in materialism. He would merely say that "emotions, instincts, degrees of talent, which are hereditary, are so because the brain of a child resembles parent stock."[56] In a sense his secretiveness was the more culpable because he also reminded himself of the persecution of early astronomers (he obviously meant Galileo) and cast himself in the martyr's role: "Must remember that if they believe and do not openly avow their belief, they do as much as to retard."[57] But he had a more comfortable policy as well, behind which there was much more than his sensitivity to his wife's piety. He cast the burden of that policy on the progress of science by taking the view that direct arguments against Christianity and theism were of no use. Enlightenment, materialistic of course, could only come in the measure (he lectured a close associate of Karl Marx), in which science progressed and its way of reasoning was absorbed by humanity at large.[58] Enlightenment could not be complete until man was seen by all as a being entirely derivable from simians.

Long before Darwin produced the *Descent*, in which he taught he had carried the cause, he was fully convinced of man's *exclusively* animal origin. He claimed in his early notebooks that "if all men were dead, then monkeys may make men. —Man makes angels." It would therefore be superficial to dismiss as stylistic bravado Darwin's declaration: "Origin of man now proved—Metaphysics must flourish. —He who understands baboon would do more toward metaphysics than Locke...Our descent then is the origin of our evil passions! —The Devil under form of Baboon is our grandfather!"[59] Clearly, Darwin could not proceed along the lines of inductive reasoning in the *Descent*, if he had reached its main conclusion more than thirty years earlier. Perhaps Darwin did not so much proceed as he was drawn. Did not Descartes, the prophet of deductive method, feel lured by some *malin génie*? Indeed, what Darwin offered was Descartes' very message, only played backward.

Jehovah dethroned

The *Descent* was a vast commentary on this message. Darwin was neither courageous nor articulate enough to spell it out in its radical form. Others quickly did it for him. The process of nature, which Darwin's theory conjured up, appeared to the German biblical critic, David Strauss, as the device which "has opened the door by which a happier coming race will cast out miracles, never to return. Everyone who knows what miracles imply will praise him, in consequence, as one of the greatest benefactors of the human race." Strauss did not have to declare that "the choice only lies between the miracle—the divine artificer—and Darwin."[64] The phrase "cast out miracles" made perfectly clear that salvation was to come to mankind because science, Darwin's science of course, had reduced to illusion the acts of One who "cast out devils." Indeed, the message of Darwin was drawn irresistibly to expression in biblical phrases turned inside out. William Kingdon Clifford, who, at the age of 25, was made professor of applied mathematics at the University College of London, showed his penetration as he summed up the thrust of Darwin's *Descent*: "Those who can read the signs of the times read in them that the Kingdom of Man is at hand."[61] So he concluded his essay, written in his last year, 1877, in the *Nineteenth Century*. No less prominent a forum, the *Quarterly Review*, in the same year also carried an essay by Clifford which concluded with this peroration: "The dim and shadowy outlines of the superhuman deity fade slowly away from before us; and as the mist of his presence floats aside, we perceive with great and greater clearness the shape of a yet grander and nobler figure—of Him who made all Gods and shall unmake them. From the dim dawn of history, and from the innermost depth of every soul, the face of our father Man looks out upon us with the fire of eternal youth in his eyes, and says, before Jehovah was, I am!"[62]

Clifford's theme was the sins committed by religion in the name of God and the pious ease with which religion, especially Catholicism, absolved sins committed against men. With heavy sarcasm Clifford assured his readers that God may forgive anyone a sin that concerns the individual himself, but has no power to forgive sins committed against others. The chiefest of such sins, according to Clifford, was the move by priests and bishops to prevent their parishioners "from setting up a public library and reading room for fear they should read Darwin's works in it." The conflict between Darwin and religions denominated by Clifford as *ultramontane,* was, in his view, irreconcilable. Such religions, Clifford wrote, undermine "the supreme allegiance of the conscience to Man," because "they seek their springs of action *ultra montes,* outside of the common experience and daily life of man."[63] By *ultra montes* Clifford clearly meant ultra physics or metaphysics. Few religions, then as now, were willing to carry proudly that label which alone fits the notion of true worship.

What, ultimately, was that supreme allegiance to man which a reading of Darwin was meant to inspire? It was, of course, no allegiance at all, insofar as allegiance implies commitment to a person or a norm. The allegiance demanded by Darwinism was simply allegiance to the absence of all norms. It beckoned toward unfathomable whirls in which one was no more than flotsom hurled round and round by the blindest of blind fates. Such is not, strictly, an interpretation, but an experience. Many have felt what a biographer of Darwin, keen on psychological depths, described as the lasting effect of his reading of the *Origin.* What that book presented was not a philosophy, not even its camouflage as agressive agnosticism, or militant atheism. What it inculcated rather was "a feeling of utter insignificance in the face of the unapprehended processes of nature . . . a sense of being aimlessly adrift in the vast universe of consciousness, among an infinity of other atoms, all struggling desperately to assert their own existence at the expense of all the others."[64]

The struggle was grim, with no quarters given. Darwin applauded the Caucasian races for having "beaten the Turkish hollow in the struggle for existence."[65] Two years before World War II, the eminent Darwinist, Sir Arthur Keith, deplored the prospect of centuries of peace.[66] For all its grimness, this struggle to life or death is merely the surface. The ultimately destructive factor in the Darwinian message is revealed in its identity with that of Rousseau. Both are a celebration of incoherence. In both cases it is no less clear that the presentation of the message of incoherence calls for continual reversals in logic, at times flagrant, often almost imperceptible. Had Darwin tried to prove much less than he actually did try, he still could not have avoided elementary *non-sequiturs* and *petitio principii* issuing, at times, in rather evident self-contradictions. Thus Darwin lapsed with increasing frequency into the Lamarckian doctrine of acquired characteristics. The most revealing of such lapses crowned the *Descent of Man*, which Darwin brought to a close with the suggestion that in the human race "after long practice virtuous tendencies may be inherited."[67]

Reversals in logic

In the same book the *non-sequiturs* were particularly prolific in the two chapters on man's intellectual faculties and moral sense. Darwin's grand conclusion: "We may trace a perfect gradation from the mind of an utter idiot, lower than that of an animal low in the scale, to the mind of Newton"[68]—was full of rhetoric, empty of logic, and void of factual evidence. Within the blissful vision of infinite gradations even a hugh difference could appear as continuity. The way a dog looked at his master, who returned home after a long absence, and the face of a man absorbed in his prayers, suggested to Darwin the same inner reality. As with any other vision, that of infinite gradations also rests on imagination, not on rigorous reasoning. When submitted to close scrutiny the vision is riddled with contradictions. Contradictions oft-noted, but rarely with this force: "an aggregate of inappreciable increments is simultaneously equated—in its cause to *nothing*, in its effect to the *whole of things*." Without appreciating one's mind one will have no appreciation of the equally forceful remark made in the same breath and about the same vision: "a logical theft is more easily committed piecemeal than wholesale. Surely it is a mean device for a philosopher to crib causation by hairs-breadths, to put it out at compound interest through all time, and then disown the debt."[69]

While it has now become clear that such policy brings the economy of even most powerful and rich nations to the brink of disaster, Darwinists for the most part still think that in their own field the same policy will not invite ultimate bankruptcy. On this score at least the anti-Darwinians were not guilty. Whatever the naiveté and the incompetence of many of them in matters scientific, they unerringly sensed two all-important points. One was the thievery which called for an absence of broad daylight and aimed at the greatest of all thefts, the one which deprives man of God. Chesterton gave the shortest and sharpest portrait of Darwinists who "suggest everywhere the grey gradations of twilight, because they believe it is the twilight of the gods."[70] The other concerns the deepest prompting against Darwinism. It did not consist, to quote Chesterton again, in dismay on seeing in a zoo one's forefathers. "It was this: that when one begins to think of man as a shifting and alterable thing, it is always easy for the strong and crafty to twist him into new shapes for all kinds of unnatural purposes."[71] Healthy instincts once more anticipated sound reasoning.

Relatively few are bothered today by thievery in matters of logic, although it is a staple feature of almost everything written on behalf of Darwinism, which is not to be equated with the instrumentality of one species in the rise of another, and certainly not with the evolutionary perspective. That lack of concern is easy to explain. Our age is dominated by the Hegelian right and left, in both of which the rise of qualities, or essential differences, is posited as the outcome of the piling of quantities upon quantities. A long series of small thefts will not, however, remain hidden in the long run. Darwin himself came to realize this. If man's mind derived from that of a monkey, or of any hypothesized missing link, whatever it may be, the conclusions of the human mind could not be more trustworthy than those arising in a monkey's mind.[72] Spencer grasped the implication of this with a cosmic sweep as he came to grips with what he called a "paralyzing thought—what if, of all this that is thus incomprehensible to us, there exists no comprehension anywhere?"[73] Darwin could never see that far. When troubled by certain vistas, he preferred to settle matters with remarks such as that "a dog might as well speculate on the mind of Newton."[74] He did not even see how heavily he relied on his own mind and on all minds which were able to perform with him two acts. One was a trickery, or the willingness to turn upside down the logic of probabilities. In Darwin's *Origin,* which he took for "one long argument,"[75] the joining of particular probabilities produced an ever greater probability and not, as it should have, an ever greater improbability. The other act was not at all ignoble. It was the act of vision, the power of the mind to see rightly or wrongly a continuous pattern despite the fact that huge lacunae—in the fossil record and elsewhere—gaped ominously for the theory.

To see in that trickery and vision, mental acts indispensable for Darwinism, a refutation of its claim about man's mind, would be to ask too much in our age unmindful of man as well as of mind. It is better to turn to topics more specific and tangible. There, too, Darwin set a pattern for myopia. One such topic is the relation between the evolution of the brain and mental functions. Within the Darwinian perspective bodily organs develop under pressure for survival. For the large size of the human brain Darwin could invoke only the pressing need for mental operations, above all, language. He merely put the cart before the horse, as Wallace pointed out to him, though somewhat tactfully, two years before the publication of the *Descent*.[76] Darwin's refusal, and that of many others after him, to take to heart Wallace's objection leaves it intact. Indeed, a hundred years later it looms larger than ever.[77] As a present-day investigator of the problem, who is certainly not disposed to see man as other than an animal, wrote: "Our brain has increased much more rapidly than any prediction based on compensations for body size would allow." Then he added sheepishly: "My conclusion is unconventional and it does reinforce an ego that we would do well to deflate. Nonetheless, our brain has undergone a true increase in size not related to the demands of our larger body. We are, indeed, smarter than we are."[78]

The debasing of intellect, as a consequence of Darwinism, could not have been put any smarter. A fragrant red-herring was once more thrown in the path of the unwary reader. He was not to worry. Smart people never do. But intelligent people know that the foregoing conclusion is only one of many which cannot be brushed aside by a smart comment. An even more telling one was reached by a leading investigator of linguistics, and especially of syntax, again of the materialist persuasion. According to N. Chomsky special neuronal integrating circuits had to exist in the brain before sentences, the essence of language, could be spoken.[79] Very recent reports of animals using language reveal that first they had to be conditioned, nay trained, for such a purpose.[80] By whom? By other animals unable yet to use language? Was man endowed with a brain suited for the art of speech only to lapse time and again into the trick of putting the cart before the horse, and do so in the name of that most specific language, science?

The size of the human brain must appear disproportionately the largest when viewed within the perspective of time in which Darwin sought the safest refuge of his theory of evolution. He felt that insensible increments could explain any development provided time was available in practically unlimited quantities. It is well to recall his dismay on learning that leading physicists of his time calculated the age of the earth at a mere 100 or so million years.[81] He was no longer alive when physicists had to revise their estimate by a factor of about fifty. Undoubtedly, a geological past measured in billions of years would have appeared for Darwin as an assurance for the eventual discovery of the missing link between men and monkeys. He would have undoubtedly believed that the "Piltdown man" put the final seal of truth to his theory. A quarter of a century after the Piltdown find turned out to be a mere hoax, it is still hard to believe that it could ever have misled the scientific community in the twentieth century. Yet the Piltdown bones were taken for almost two generations for an evidence worth being enshrined as a sacred milestone of the cultural heritage. "Amongst British authorities," we read in the 14th edition of the *Encyclopaedia Britannica* (1929–33) "there is now agreement that the skull [human] and the jaw [chimpanzee] are parts of the same individual and that the brain, as revealed by casts taken from the interior of the skull, is human in its size and in all its characters." The Piltdown man, together with the Java man, were not so much chief witnesses to the reality of the missing link, as the same encyclopedia and many other distinguished sources would have it,[82] but rather constructs of wishful thinking to which men of science are not immune.

Half-a-century later the fossil landscape certainly looks very different. The least important in this respect is the geographical shift. The cradle of mankind and of the missing link passed from Asia to Africa. The really important shift is the increase of the human past from about a hundred thousand years to between 1 and 3 million years, a development most disconcerting for Darwinism.

The finding of genuinely human-like fossils (with tools and ashes, the product of fire-making) in the ever more distant past drastically shortens the time available for the explosively fast growth of the brain in order to serve as a tool for humanness. This shortening of much-needed time comes to the fore in most roundabout ways. On the evolutionary timetable, as estimated on the basis of change in certain albumin protein substances, the divergence point between chimpanzees and man is not older than about 4 million years. This would leave a mere million years, a fleeting moment, for the doubling of the brain which is still difficult to imagine if the divergence point is set, on another basis, at about 25 million years. The situation should seem desperate for Darwinists if the divergence point or missing link is embodied in the recently found *australopithecus afarensis* estimated to be 4 million years old. Perhaps this is what was in the back of the mind of Leakey when to the question, whether the new species—represented most memorably by a fairly complete female skeleton (with erect posture, small pelvis and skull) called "Lucy"—is the missing link, he replied: "I believe that the common ancestor has not yet been found."[83] Leakey could hardly be unaware of the saying making the rounds among anthropologists tired of a long and vain search for that ancestor: "Man is the missing link between anthropoid apes and human beings."[84]

Apes and ethics

Intellect is only one chief distinction of being truly human. Another is good will, co-operation, which should seem even more mysterious than intellect in an existence which, within the Darwinian perspective is all "red in tooth and claw." Within that perspective nothing is more logical than to consider human aggressiveness as a genetically imposed feature of human behavior, a factor to trap man forever in disastrous wars. Man's simian ancestor has long been looked upon as a "killer ape." But was Cain more aboriginal than Abel? Was man first a hunter and then a gatherer? According to some good recent evidence the contrary seems to be true. Leakey and his co-worker, R. Lewin, certainly startled the world of evolutionary science by their claim that first came the sharing of food and co-operation. Hunting had to come afterwards as a far less effective means of sustenance. The "people of the lake," as Leakey and Lewin called their primordial humans,[85] achieved dominance over other hominids through the fact that they were a better species in an unmistakably moral sense.

Any recognition of man as a moral being strikes at the very foundation of Darwinist evolutionism. To be sure, its chief believers keep asserting that they have succeeded in deriving values from facts and they continue to obtain prominent forums in which to reassure their fellow believers and persuade the unwary that the impossible is possible. Their claims concerning the derivation of ethics from mere behavior is rarely presented with the graphic concreteness of "Termites and Telescopes," the title of the second Bronowski lecture.[86] To hear the claim that, given enough time, termites would come up with a telescope and use it to good advantage should make even the unwary sit up in disbelief. The claim, boastfully voiced in our times by Bronowski, that he has succeeded in deriving values from facts, triggers no suspicion even among many who should know better. In fact, the very motivation behind efforts aimed at achieving such a feat runs contrary to the basic tenets of Darwinism. Did not Darwin warn himself, to no avail of course, that in discoursing about evolution, the valuational terms, 'lower' and 'higher', ought to be avoided?[87] The gospel of the "ascent of man" as preached by Bronowski with the help both of the press and of world-wide television, is an old shoe stitched together with Darwinian inconsistencies. A better book with the same title was produced almost a hundred years ago.[88] A better book because its author learned from no less a Darwinist than T. H. Huxley, a point which, for all its importance, Bronowski did not report.

In its heyday the Romanes lectures were certainly a prominent occasion. The lecturer for 1893, T. H. Huxley, was of a prominence which has not diminished since his death in 1895. Nor decreased the significance of his lecture, "Evolution and Ethics," in which he acknowledged that while one could speak of the evolution of ethics, it made no sense to speak of the ethics of evolution: "The practice of that which is ethically best—what we call goodness or virtue—involves a course of conduct which, in all its respects, is opposed to that which leads to success in the cosmic struggle for existence . . . . Moral precepts are directed to the end of curbing the cosmic process and reminding the individual of his duty to the community, to the protection and influence of which he owes, if not existence itself, at least the life of something better than a brutal savage."[89] Rousseau would have gulped. If Darwinists did, it was only because they forgot that Darwin said much the same when he spoke of moral conscience as a dictate telling man to go counter to social instinct.[90] Instead of instinct he would have said genes or chromosomes, had they been known by then.

The reality of moral dictates, of altruism, of love has remained for Darwinism a major stumbling block. A principal though unwitting witness in this respect is none other than E. O. Wilson, chief spokesman for sociobiology, the latest and most sweeping form of Darwinism. For if it is true that sociobiology has for its "central theoretical question: how can altruism, which by definition reduces personal fitness, possibly evolve by natural selection,"[91] then clearly no progress has been made since Darwin. It was he who offered first for solution the idea, if not the expression, of "kin selection," the favorite device in this respect of sociobiologists. He preferred, he said, to have for his forefather "that old baboon, who, descending from the mountains, carried away in triumph his young comrade from a crowd of astonished dogs," rather than "from a savage . . . who offers up bloody sacrifices . . . . "[92] Darwinists for the most part still fail to recognize with T. H. Huxley in ethics something which should seem both an obvious fact and also an inescapable contradiction for Darwinism. On both counts ethical force, to recall Huxley's words, is "the checking of the cosmic process at every step" and a substitution for it of another—the end of which is not the survival of those who may happen to be the fittest . . . but of those who are ethically the best."[93] Darwinists have no answer to this dilemma because the only answer—the recognition of a spiritual order in man who is more than mere matter—cannot come within their ken, a ken constructed to the specifications of strict materialism. Thus those who refuse to acknowledge the dualism of man are condemned to side with the dualism of the Manicheans of old who conjure up two ultimate and equal forces: one remorseless, another good—caught in eternal antagonism.

The same contradiction, when translated into the dualism of blind versus purposeful, haunts the Darwinists no less while making them oblivious to another fact, although it is a fact within the reach of an elementary reflection on what they themselves are doing. Their work is a life-long commitment to the purpose of proving that there is no purpose. Every Darwinist is a living refutation of a philosophy, Darwinism, for which purpose is non-existent. For whatever the Darwinian claim that no biological organization can be shown to have developed for a purpose and under a directive agency, at least one organism or species, and hardly the least important, man, is engaged day in and day out in the most varied and most spectacularly purposeful activities. Man's recently acquired ability to mold his genetic storehouse for a purpose is unexplainable within the Darwinian perspective. The failure of Darwinists to take seriously the fact that they are acting for a purpose, witnessed by their zealous crusades, is a sign of a schizophrenia which is of a piece with their resolve to consider only part of man, his body, while ignoring his mind.

The faith of Darwinists

Respectability of Darwinian philosophy has a lively resource in the contemporary slighting of man's intellectuality, which is also discredited through self-styled rationalistic trends in philosophy, be they variations on phenomenalism, logical positivism, or empiricism. Those who truly value the human intellect have been intimidated, in such an atmosphere, from using it as a prime proof that, for all his animality, man is very much more than an animal. Yet admirers of man's mind stand on vastly firmer ground than do their opponents. On what ground could a mere animal resort to what Huxley called "an act of philosophical faith," to secure credibility to a pivotal point of Darwinism, the emergence of life out of non-living matter? How could a mere animal resort to what Huxley called "analogical reasoning" and use it as a substitute for factual evidence? Clearly, man's mental powers demanded a better account than the epiphenomenalism proposed by Huxley. He had little right to paddle in such shallows after he declared that "belief, in the scientific sense of the word, is a serious matter, and needs strong foundations."[94] The ease with which he proposed epiphenomenalism as the explanation of the brain-mind relationship, and the ease with which it was received in his camp hardly suggest profundity of thought. Sophisticated shallowness (especially evident in the so-called identity theory of the mind-body relationship) characterizes most efforts to avoid dualism. To make matters worse, dualism is often equated with its Cartesian form which is surely unworthy of serious consideration.

When Darwinists examine dualism (which they usually skim) at any depth, the mind-body relationship acquires a perspective which today, just as in Huxley's time, is distinctly theological. That perspective, much broader than that of either mind or body or both, was the last, as Huxley put it, of four possible ontological hypotheses. The four differed according to whether they involved no unknown, or one, or two, or three unknowns, or rather unknowables. By 'unknowables' Huxley meant, in this context, not only mind, but also matter, and, of course, God. The first of the four possibilities was atheism on Berkelian principles which, being solipsism, contained no unknowable, at least for the knowing self. The possibility with one unknowable was materialism or pantheism, "according as you turn it heads or tails," in the words of Huxley, who opted for materialism. The third possibility with two unknowables, matter and mind, was the product of speculators "*incertae sedis*," that is, of most unreliable speculators, a description certainly befitting Cartesian dualists. The fourth possibility, with three unknowables—God, soul (mind), and matter—was in Huxley's words the position of "orthodox theologians."[95]

Unfortunately, the number of such theologians who, precisely because of their *knowledge* of matter, do know soul as well as God, has considerably diminished. Their less orthodox kind may gather something of the consistency of that fourth position by reflecting not so much on the three other positions as on Huxley's remark introducing them. There Huxley gave a taste of the utter scepticism in which one lands once God as the ultimate in intelligibility and being is put beyond the pale. To begin with, Huxley claimed that a universe, in which twice two made not four but five, was possible. Second, he admitted that, although he opted for materialism, he knew just as little what matter was as he knew nothing about mind. Possibly he did not realize that his predicament had already been stated in one short line by an older contemporary of his, Thomas H. Key: "What is mind? No matter. What is matter? Never mind."[96]

Utter scepticism is the end product of the reasoning implied in Darwinism. Beneath that scepticism there lurks a sort of pseudo world-view which, because it implies the denial of consistency, is neither a view nor an acceptable theoretical account of the "world"—the totality of consistently interacting entities, which is the only world worth being called a universe required by and useful for science. This is not to say that Bertrand Russell, who once poured scepsis on "all of man's hopes, fears, loves and beliefs,"[97] as the accidental collision of atoms, was utterly consistent. He did not deny consistency to the atoms. Russell was, however, consistent when he opposed Julian Huxley's portrayal of the Darwinian world in rosy hues. Under the circumstances, such cosmic optimism demanded, in Russell's view, greater faith than the Christian creed itself. The grandson of T. H. Huxley certainly gave evidence of a robust faith as he did his very best to restore hopeful vistas shattered by his grandfather's candid statement on the true relation between ethical outlook and Darwinism.[98] Even apart from its broader vistas, Darwinism as a scientific research program is staked on the faith of its protagonists. It was a professor of zoology at Cambridge, James Gray, fully committed to the evolutionary view, who declared: "No amount of argument, or clever epigram, can disguise the inherent improbability of orthodox evolutionary theory; but most biologists feel it is better to think in terms of improbable events than not to think at all." That faith is indeed the ultimate sustaining force in question is equally the gist of Gray's rejoinder to Huxley's reply: "None of the works to which Prof. Huxley refers, or appears to have in mind, gives me reason to believe that a conclusive demonstration of the fact that certain things can happen is necessarily a proof that they have happened."[99]

Though not a botanist, Gray could not be unaware of the fact that the realm of plants presents no less grave questions for Darwinism than does the realm of animals. Yet he and others cling to Darwinism as a method in spite of their keen awareness of its serious inadequacies. They do so for a very good reason. Science could not acquire its wings until it had eliminated questions of purpose from its method. The establishment of quantitative correlations is the sole purpose of science and the sole guarantee that it can become predictive and verifiable. The scientist investigating sound is as entitled to ignore aesthetic considerations as the composer is entitled to ignore the mathematical equations governing the propagation of sound. To ignore is one thing, to deny is another. By failing to heed this distinction Darwinists become Darwinian philosophers who revel in the denial of logic and values. They also remain blissfully unmindful of the fact that as a scientific theory Darwinism is just as incomplete and revisable as any other scientific theory. The pressure of environment and the slight genetic changes ever at work in every organism propagating itself, may or may not be sufficient to explain all steps in the transformation of one species into another, let alone of a family into another, to say nothing of phylae and kingdoms. Those who dogmatically give the affirmative answer are still lacking something essential to the scientific spirit.

Christians and Darwinism

The spirit of science implies also bold vision, though not the kind of boldness which makes one forget that vision is not observational evidence. While some time before Darwin the vision of an immense past was gaining in acceptance, (indeed, belief in evolution itself had long been conceded), it was through Darwin and Darwinism that the parameter of time became an indispensable framework for understanding. In view of the dignity which time received through Christ's coming in the fullness of time, Christians should not have been upset by the new trend to understand in terms of evolution. Again, in view of their belief in the Word made flesh, Christians should have been more open to the flood of experiments involving living matter, a flood generated by Darwinism. In view of their professed belief in the goodness of matter and the sacredness of life, they should, perhaps, have more highly esteemed hosts of guinea pigs of all kinds that died in "Darwinian" laboratories so that man may live longer and proved thereby that he was their kin.

Had Christians been deeply steeped in the understanding provided by their faith, they might, from the start, have distinguished the gold from the straw in evolutionary theory. All too often they even failed to notice the huge piles of straw. Why is it, one may ask, that Christian analysis of Darwinian evolution places so little emphasis on the weakness of a view which turns time into a hopeless treadmill? Did not Huxley himself conjure up the vision of a meaningless evolution in which higher and lower were indistinguishable precisely because moving into the future was not, in the Darwinian perspective, different from receding into the past?[100] Should not Christian scholars have set forth in great detail, and long before Huxley spoke, that the cyclic view of existence was a distinctive feature not only of Hindu thought, but of all non-Christian cultures, and that in all of them science suffered a stillbirth?[101] Why was it that so many Christian scholars of recent times failed to remember that the great clash between nascent Christianity and Hellenistic culture came over the question whether life, including the redeeming life of Christ, was a once-and-for-all proposition, or whether life was mere flotsom on the unfathomable cyclic currents of blind cosmic force? The confrontation provoked by Darwinism was in essence a replay of some old, though fundamental stances.

Christians cannot, of course, be expected to display superhuman insight at every new turn taken by intellectual fashion. Nor can they be held accountable for Darwin's motivation, which was not so much scientific as countermetaphysical. The inept philosophizing of Darwin and Darwinians is not of Christian provenance. Christians are certainly not the source of the stereotyped descriptions of Darwin as the genius who staked everything on natural selection. Compared to another issue, natural selection was relatively unimportant for Darwin. That other issue was special creation. Darwin left no doubt as to the lesser importance he attributed to natural selection. His statements[102] are, however, misleading if taken at face value, namely, that his overriding concern was the overthrow of the special creation of each and every species. It is safer to say that Darwin wanted to discredit the notion of creation as such. He realized that creation and evolution are not mutually exclusive, but materialism and creation certainly exclude one another.

At any rate, Darwin was not willing to tolerate the prospect of a special creation in any sense, not even in respect to man's intellectual faculties. For him, as he put it in the *Descent*, "man in the rudest state in which he now exists is the most dominant animal that has ever appeared on this earth." The paragraph which begins with this phrase ends as follows: "I cannot therefore *understand*, how it is that Mr. Wallace maintains that 'natural selection could only have endowed the savage with a brain little superior to that of the ape'."[103] The chief trouble with this phrase related neither to Mr. Wallace nor to natural selection, but to Darwin's failure to catch even a glimpse of what is implied in the process of *understanding*. Such and similar statements of Darwin fully justify the comment that "Darwin was no crude leveler down to origins. He may more readily be accused of making animals too human than of making men too animal."[104] In sum, he glorified the ape and this also meant the debunking of creation.

In the process Darwin debunked thought itself, although he resorted to thought as the ultimate guarantee that the vast array of facts he marshalled did not speak falsely: "He who is not content to look, like a savage, at the phenomena of nature as disconnected, cannot any longer believe that man is the work of a separate act of creation."[105] Darwin did not as much as suspect that this very ability of man, which is not possessed by the "savage" and makes science possible, was the irrefragable evidence that a special creation did indeed take place when it came to the mind of man. This is why the hostility of Christians to Darwin's hostility to Christianity should not appear unreasonable. Christians certainly cannot be made the principal carriers of unreasonableness when reasons given for siding with Darwinism reveal matters very distinct from reasoning. Aldous Huxley is a priceless witness in this respect. In speaking about the favor which the philosophy of meaninglessness found with him and with his generation, he candidly identified that favor as a licence for sexual indulgence. His claim that Darwinism when first formulated, was not used as "justification for sexual indulgence,"[106] suggests that subsequently it was. The mere evocation of the slogan, "the family is evolving," a slogan so dear to sociologists and psychiatrists, to say nothing of behaviorists and social engineers, should be enough of a proof. Even more important should seem Huxley's description of meaninglessness. It consists in assigning meaning to parts while denying meaning to the whole.[107] Darwinism perfectly fits this description. Engrossed in observable parts of man, it grows insensitive to what is always unobservable, the whole man, a reality nonetheless. Darwinists resentful of such metaphysical intrusions should perhaps remind themselves of Claude Bernard's remark that he never saw life.[108] He did not doubt its existence although he could only see its disconnected parts. There, too, metaphysics provided the whole, that is, the vision of organic life.

One of those parts to which Darwinism assigns meaning is the mechanism of evolution. Darwinism did so even when the mechanism (genetic variation) was still unknown, and it certainly does so today when genetic engineering is turning into a frighteningly effective tool. Frightening because the self-imposed blindness of Darwinists concerning purpose and mind locks them into fearsome perspectives. The latest evidence in this connection is *Genes, Mind and Culture* whose co-author, E. O. Wilson, a Harvard specialist in ants, made himself a name by pontificating on man.[109] Wilson now claims, with the help of Charles Lumsden, a mathematician, that fairly rapid genetic transmutation of the entire society is possible. On finding that the time in question is only 30 generations, they noticed with no sign of unease that it is equivalent to a thousand years and blithely called their finding a "thousand-year rule."[110] Did they remember Hitler and his advocacy of exactly that rule, and on Darwinian grounds to boot?

A planet of apes

For their apparently unconcerned consistency Lumsden and Wilson deserve credit and gratitude. Nothing is more valuable than clear, if not clean, air. What is truly reprehensible in the whole affair is the indignation of some self-styled humanists who, on seeing Nazi ideology raise its head from beneath the cloak of sociobiology, raise hue and cry. It is indeed a tragic irony that those who battled valiantly Nazi onslaughts provided so many spokesmen for the philosophy of Darwinism, with its derision of the Christian teaching of creation and man. They all seem curiously forgetful of the once-famed message which Bernard Shaw addressed to his fellow Anglo-Saxons in the wake of World War I, that first step in implementing the suicide of the Western World.

Few could remain ignorant at that time of the Preface to Shaw's *Heartbreak House*. Shaw had Darwinism in mind as he located the source of cultural breakdown in the belief that salvation was to come through science. As is well known Darwin would never have written his *Descent of Man* had he learned soon enough that his *Origin of Species* had already been carried to its full logic in Ernst Haeckel's *History of Creation*.[111] More than that is not needed by a way of introduction to Shaw's words: "We taught Prussia this religion; and Prussia bettered our instruction so effectively that we presently found ourselves confronted with the necessity of destroying Prussia to prevent Prussia destroying us. And that has just ended in each destroying the other to an extent doubtfully reparable in our time."[112] Shaw was fortunate in that he could not foresee a mankind sitting on the nuclear powder keg. Unfortunately, Shaw could appear novel only because man was not willing to learn. Long before Shaw, Pascal called attention to the danger in the lopsided policy which emphasizes man's equality with the brutes while blinding him to his superiority over them.

Instead of evoking, however briefly, the image of mankind blowing itself to bits, it would seem more helpful to cast a glance at the contemporary approach to man. If encyclopedias are an indication of prevailing preferences, one facet in them will appear very revealing. Conspicuously absent from them is any entry for Man as such. This is certainly the case with encyclopedias written mainly for Anglo-Saxon ambience, the cradle and most fertile soil for Darwinism. Those encyclopedias contain articles on evolution, anthropology, family, procreation, education, psychology, language, and even on intelligence, while Man as such is ignored.[113] The pattern is of a piece with the philosophy of ultimate meaninglessness in which the partial aspects are found meaningful, but never the whole.

Man is rarely, if ever, spoken of by Darwinists as a glorified ape, but he is certainly not more for them, if this is to be judged by publications, academic or popular, which receive immediate notice and wide publicity. Such is a furtive bargain and a most disastrous one, in keeping with transactions carried out under the counter. Cultural collapse is unwittingly invited through that intellectual transaction in which man himself becomes mere merchandise and the planet earth is turned into an abode for glorified apes. Whereas even Darwinists, when thinking as men and not as Darwinists, find unpalatable being classified as upper-grade simians, the average educated man readily accepts this classification when marketed by zealous salesmen of Darwinism in such inspirational wrappings as the "identity of man," the "uniqueness of man," the "ascent of man" and the like. They are so many devices to deceive the customers. Nietzsche at least did not intend to fool his readers when he said, "Man is more of an ape than any of the apes."[114] Such is certainly the case when man takes it lightly that he is a man.*

---

* It would be a mistake to consider the high tides of creationism, which periodically wash over the United States (this most receptive soil for social and other extensions of Darwinism), as a backlash of blind faith surging in the wake of pure reason. True, only the blindness induced by the radical separation of faith from reason would insist on the individual creation of each and every species, and that the age of the universe must be measured in a few thousand years. Yet constant meditation on the Bible is the most effective way to keep the supremely rational consciousness of *purpose* in focus. Even that arch-enemy of Christianity and the Bible, Nietzsche, cast an unwitting vote on behalf of such meditation when he remarked that "he who knows the *why* can bear with almost any *how*."

Rightful resistance to the wilder claims of crusading creationists would have kept its balance if highly-publicized spokesmen for Darwinism had frankly and frequently admitted that science, even Darwinism, deals only with the *how*. They seem to feel that such admissions would be fatal to that popular brand of Darwinism (which all too often masks a fierce countermetaphysics) if they amplified on their admission that "we [Darwinists] have persecuted dissenters, resorted to catechism, and tried to extend our authority to a moral sphere where it has no force . . . ." (S. J. Gould, *Ever Since Darwin*, p. 146). Although the same author declared that "no opposition exists between science and religion" (*New York Times*, Jan. 12, 1982, p. A15, col. 3), he specified neither the religion, nor the science. He also sidestepped the question whether man, once reduced to quantities, can have religion (or even science), as he argued throughout his *Mismeasure of Man* (1981) that a single quantitative parameter is not enough to evaluate man's intelligence.

Darwinism as a countermetaphysics was again too lightly touched on when the President of the Royal Society, Sir Andrew Huxley, admitted (see *Supplement to Royal Society News*, Issue 12, Nov.' 1981, p. v.) that Darwinists have "too often swept under the carpet the biggest problem in biology, the existence of consciousness." They did so, Sir Andrew should have added, because Darwinism made them insensitive to the significance of the sense of purpose and turned their very purposeful work, and themselves, into an interesting subject for study.

Such a view on the conflict of creationists and scientists may be too evenhanded to be newsworthy. Its capsule formulation, which I sent to *TIME* following a telephone interview in February, 1981, remains unpublished: "The conflict arises from the clash of two extremist camps, both dedicated to a noble aim and bringing alike discredit to it. The creationists aim at a restoration of the sense of existence through impregnating young people's minds with the biblical creation story which they expose to ridicule by taking literally all its statements. Their antagonists want to secure the sacred rights of scientific investigation which they equate with materialism, a claim as ridiculous as it is also erosive of all sense of purpose."

The reading of the Bible, ecclesiastical history is a witness, can produce fanatics by the score—so many sad subjects for study. No less sad a story is that scientific program in which, to recall a memorable indictment of the exclusivity of scientific method, the mind-body mystery of man becomes "a calculating machine in the service of a machine of pleasure." If followed consistently, such an exclusivity may justify, as Bourget's *Le disciple* (1889) illustrates, the luring of others into suicide so that this gruesome act might be observed with "scientific" detachment. Science can produce its own brand of fanaticism, a point worth pondering in an age which has at its disposal the scientific means of global suicide.

III

UNCONQUERABLE MAN

"By space the universe encompasses and swallows me up like a dot; by thought I encompass the universe."
—Pascal, *Pensées* No. 265

Science as man's conquests

The phrase, "unconquerable man," is not meant to be another encomium on the human race. Dictionaries of quotations are already bursting with praises of man. If they have any value, it lies in their ability to stand up to some test, mostly aesthetic and philosophical. Sophocles' words, "wonders are many, but none, none is more wondrous than man,"[1] usually remind us of the countless wonders which mankind owes to the artists and sages of ancient Greece. Protagoras, a contemporary of Sophocles, hardly pleased the great philosophers of ancient Greece with his statement that "man is the measure of all things." Perhaps they sensed that, if true, the statement would put an end to wonderment about anything.[2] Many modern philosophers would be pleased with Protagoras' statement as it has the ring of science. Were they to have their way, the phrase, "unconquerable man" would have to be subjected to a scientific test in order to prove its value. The idea should seem particularly attractive at a time like ours when the growth of science goes forward at an explosive rate. Over ninety percent of those who can be called scientists lived in this century.[3] Science, through its industrial applications, has become the largest employer. Last but not least, science has made far greater conquests in our century than in any century before.

Quantitative terms may not give the best idea of the significance of a conquest but even in this respect the scientific conquests achieved by man in the 20th century are spectacular. Around 1900 the best resolution of microscopes, about a thousandth of a millimeter, was the limit of man's conquest of the very small.[4] Since an atom is ten thousand times smaller, it was still respectable around 1900 to doubt the existence of atoms. Today the conquest of the realm of atoms is history. And so is the conquest of the realm of the nucleus, which is as much smaller than an atom as atoms are smaller than grains of sand, or bits of matter still visible to the naked eye. The present frontier of the conquest of the very small, or of the very structure of matter, is the realm of quarks, gluons, and even more esoteric subparticles such as massive neutrinos. The conquest, however spectacular, is far from over. While new big accelerators are being installed, far bigger ones are already on the drawing boards and some gigantic ones are dreamed about by particle physicists.[5] The conquest of the very small is far from being complete, although it has already proved man to be the conqueror of matter to an astonishing degree. He can tap its innermost energies and produce materials with fabulous properties.

The realm of the very large has been the scene of no less spectacular conquests by science. Around 1900 it was a generally accepted view that the Milky Way was perhaps forever to remain the explorable part of the universe, although its boundaries were at best a matter of guesswork. Spiral nebulae, of which thousands had been catalogued by 1900, were believed to be much smaller systems than the Milky Way and subordinate to it. The universe was believed to consist of two parts, one infinite and unfathomable, surrounding a small observable part, spherical in shape, whose main plane was the Milky Way.[6] Before long this neat and cozy structure began to crumble. A few years before the 100-inch telescope at Mount Wilson was inaugurated in 1918, stars known as Cepheid variables were found to be very useful for estimating very large distances. The sighting of a Cepheid variable in the Andromeda nebula followed within a decade. The universe, until 1925 a universe of stars, suddenly emerged as a universe of galaxies.[7]

The distance of Andromeda, 2 million light years, which at first astonished the world of science, soon appeared puny. At the same time it was found that the farther away was a galaxy, the greater a shift toward the red was shown by its spectrum. In other words, as the conquest of space witnessed its greatest expansion, the universe itself was found to be expanding. Some, Hubble, for instance, who with Humason formulated in 1929 the distance-velocity relationship,[8] could never bring themselves to believe the expansion of the universe. It contradicted long-cherished beliefs, which, as will be seen, were themselves laden with contradictions. Today, the greatest observed red shifts indicate distances of over 10 billion light years, where galaxies move with two-thirds of the speed of light. The 94-inch telescope which will be placed in orbit in 1985 is expected to increase the observable volume of the universe by a factor of about 350.[9] The story of the conquest of new continents would be repeated again on an immensely vaster scale. As new lands were penetrated surprising novelties in fauna and flora were spotted.[10] Quasars, pulsars, and black holes are some of the novel species discovered in recent years in far-away space. Only the unexpected can really be expected in the continuing drama of man's conquest of space in the remainder of the twentieth century and in the century to come.

The universe conquered

Interesting as this story is and instructive as it is about man's ability to conquer, it contains no details or data which would suggest that as man conquered space he gave evidence of being unconquerable. Of course, that story about man's conquering larger and larger domains of outer space is by far the less important part of man's unrelenting effort to come to grips with the universe. The far more important part of the story is the fact that for the first time in history man was able to conquer the universe. Man did not achieve this through experimental wizardry, nor can he ever do it in such a way, immensely far as he may look or go into outer space. Being part of the universe, man cannot take up a post beyond the universe, so as to overlook it as though he were its conqueror. The conquest by man of the universe is as more subtle as the conceptual grasp of an object is superior to its being held in one's hands. Conceptual grasp, or the ability to think, is of course much older than science. Modern science was not needed to prove through the scientific ingenuity of man that man was more than anything sensory, nay all sensory. To anyone sensitive to philosophical depth, modern science adds nothing to the validity of Pascal's observation about man's unconquerability by matter and even by its totality, the universe. The heart of that observation, repeated to the point of boredom, though never boring in itself, is that man, though feeble as a reed, is nonetheless a thinking reed.[11] Unless one is sensitive enough to marvel at the ability of man to think, no conviction will be carried by the contrast between man, who knows that a mere drop of water can extinguish him, and the whole universe which knows nothing of its ability, or of the ability of even its smallest part, to crush man in a split-second.

Still, modern science can be extremely helpful in restoring that philosophical sensitivity which has been almost completely discredited by a now very lame logical positivism and its limping offshoots parading as scientific philosophies.[12] That the so-called scientific philosophies should receive their sharpest rebuff from twentieth-century science will surprise only those who look at science through lenses ground to the specifications of logical positivism. The chief of those rebuffs is the recently-acquired ability of science to discourse, in a manner free of contradictions, on the interaction of all matter. This ability is nothing short of "handling," so to speak, the universe itself insofar as it is the totality of consistently interacting material entities.[13] Science, or rather man through his science, now can, in a metaphorical sense, hold the universe in his hands, just as a conqueror lays his hands on his booty.

The picture, or the conquest it portrays, is not complete. General Relativity provided for the first time in scientific history a consistent cosmology only insofar as gravitational interaction is concerned. A Unified Field Theory, valid for all interactions—gravitational, electromagnetic, weak, nuclear and perhaps some others—still is to be worked out. The success of General Relativity shows nonetheless that the idea of the universe is not, as Kant wanted us to believe, a bastard product of the metaphysical craving of the intellect, but a notion indispensable for science. Moreover, the modern science of cosmology blocks the escape route of Neo-Kantians of all varieties who think that by raising that bastard product to the dignity of a regulatory idea,[14] the metaphysical sting will have been taken out of it. Contrary to their belief, the notion of the universe as needed by science is a notion as much subject to empirical and quantitative verifications and corrections as are all other scientific notions whose validity is not questioned.

Through the human acumen implied in General Relativity, the universe has been sighted in its reality, as a concrete tangible entity which can be sized up and whose structure can be investigated. A tangible entity it is, no less than a dress on a clothier's rack. Like a dress or any artifact, the universe has a measure, a size, a shape, a very specific provenance and in a subtle sense also a prize. Dressmakers would smile understandingly on hearing that the universe even has a curvature. For better or for worse the curvature of the cosmos is not easily visualizable. A very specific figure it certainly is.[15] In view of this it should matter little whether the total amount of matter which constitutes the universe is infinite or not. If it is finite, it certainly suggests something strikingly metaphysical by its very limitedness even to those insensitive to, or unfamiliar with, metaphysics. In fact, patently metaphysical were the shock-waves triggered by Einstein's lectures in 1922 at the Sorbonne where he insisted, before a stunned audience of scientists and philosophers, that General Relativity leads to a universe in which the total amount of matter is finite in such a way as to produce a close spherical network of possible lines of motion, the new definition of space.[16]

Einstein may have been wrong on the finiteness of total matter, but it hardly matters. There are, as Einstein himself had already pointed out, conceivable geometries, such as the one corresponding to a cylindrical space,[17] in which an infinite amount of matter can be accommodated without incurring the so-called gravitational paradox, or infinite gravitational potential at any point. Whatever its infinity, a cylindrical universe is an entity which declares by its very specificity that it is not necessarily what it is. No different is the case with other, scientifically permissible aggregates of an infinite amount of matter. A universe in which all permissible paths of motion follow hyperbolic lines[18] is just as specific, although the matter that can be allocated along those lines can be infinite. The question, whether the total matter of the universe is infinite or finite, has its answer in the measurement of a finite quantity, the mean density of matter in cosmic spaces. Its value has been the subject of continual refinements for the past fifty years or so.[19] It is a very specific value nonetheless, the kind of value which alone is meaningful in science.

The specificity of the universe which makes its notion so spectacularly valid for scientists—and for philosophers truly knowledgeable about science—has emerged not only in space but in time as well. Shortly after Einstein published in 1917 the final or cosmological installment of his General Relativity,[20] his world model was proved by de Sitter to be unstable, that is, subject to expanding. It was not until ten years later that, on the basis of that model, the recessional velocity of galaxies was predicted by the abbé Lemaître.[21] The simultaneous formulation by Hubble and Humason of the distance-velocity law for galaxies provided an experimental seal on a newly-emerging aspect of the universe which carried a blunt message. A being like man, so sensitive to his limitations set by time, could not but be struck by the fact that the universe was no less time-conditioned. As in the case of man, in the case of the universe too, existence in time is a powerful reminder of transitoriness or contingency. Man, if he is sensitive enough philosophically, also should be struck by the fact that while the universe knows nothing of its transitoriness, man is able to perceive not only his own transitoriness but also that of the universe. The topic has a grandeur to which only a Pascal could do full justice.

It has been through the specificity of cosmic time that man has obtained his deepest insight into the enormously specific structure of the universe. Such has been, however, a much delayed outcome. No sooner had Lemaître's paper come to the notice of the astronomical world than efforts were made to blunt its patently metaphysical edge.[22] The popularity of the idea of an oscillating universe, for which there is allegedly no time limit, should be seen in this light.[23] Curiously, hardly anybody took note of a page in the classic work on relativistic cosmology by Tolman who showed as early as 1934 that even an oscillating universe was limited in time, because its periods of oscillation had to be shorter with each period completed.[24] The steady-state theory of the universe, which even apart from all experimental tests should seem too arbitrary to deserve more than a fleeting mention, was another effort to exorcize the limitedness of the universe in time.[25] At any rate, with the discovery by A. A. Penzias and R. W. Wilson in 1965 of the 3°K cosmic background radiation,[26] the steady-state theory lost its last shreds of respectability.[27] The big-bang theory, insofar as it implies a once-and-for-all expansion for the universe, is still the most reliable of all cosmological models. Of course, advocates of an oscillating universe keep looking for any straw that would indicate the existence of a so-called "missing matter."[28] A tellingly materialist counterpart of the missing link,[29] that missing matter may turn the actual expansion of the universe into a contraction, but still, as was noted above, it cannot give eternity to the universe. One may legitimately wish that this purely scientific point be duly noted by those who today view in the best possible light observational data about massive neutrinos, which may provide that missing matter. Perhaps it would be too much to expect them to be utterly candid about their materialistic motivations in looking at these and other data, among which the 3°K cosmic background radiation is of unique significance.

The story of the 3°K cosmic background radiation is well known through able popularizations. Possibly the best of them has as title, *The First Three Minutes,*[30] a first-rate misnomer. It can easily create the impression that science can specify the first moment of physical interactions, let alone the very moment of creation.[31] It is also misleading because it draws attention away from what should seem to be most significant in the 3°K radiation. That radiation is a supreme evidence that speculations about the primordial structuring of the universe[32] are on the right track in more than one sense. No track could be straighter, narrower, more specific, or, from the point of view of man, more consequential. The track leads to a primordial condition of the universe which can be told in a few lines, almost in a few words, illustrating the stunning power of the mind to conquer the universe. That it takes only a few words stands to reason. The more specific an entity is, the fewer words it takes to identify it. The identity tag for the universe in its primordial state need not contain more than the following data: one proton, one neutron, and one electron for every 1000 million photons, and the whole conglomerate at a temperature of about a hundred billion degrees.[33] Such are the necessary parameters for the genesis of all chemical elements forming the actual universe. Had any of those parameters been different, however slightly, the formation of the actual set of elements could not have taken place, the universe would not be what it is, and we humans could not be part of it as our physical make-up is based on that very same set.

The anthropic principle

Such is the background to the emergence in modern cosmology of the so-called anthropic principle.[34] In itself it merely states that the universe has from its earliest stage been on an evolutionary track along which alone was the emergence of man ultimately possible. The anthropic principle certainly does not mean that modern cosmology has shown the emergence of man to be a necessary outcome of the primordial mix. The anthropic principle is, however, certainly indicative of the extent to which man is able to conquer the universe by his knowledge of it. Yet this knowledge is so specifically objective as to constitute a proof that man cannot be conquered by the universe. Man certainly would suffer his worst defeat at the hands of the universe if it could be shown that what is known of the universe is merely man's imposing of his own stamp on reality. In this case the anthropic principle would indeed be the highest form of anthropocentrism. Since anthropocentrism is the worst disservice to man, once harnessed in its service the anthropic principle would turn into a misanthropy principle. The specificity of the universe strongly discourages a view of the anthropic principle as a harbinger of anthropocentrism. Such a view, as will be seen shortly, is also vitiated by a theoretical consideration. The anthropic principle has an all-important epistemological significance and carries by the same token a far-reaching message for an anthropology which has the courage to face head-on the question: what is man?

The anthropic principle is the very opposite of anthropocentrism, precisely because it eliminates the most sophisticated form of subjectivism, embodied in a priori theories about man's knowing the world. This is not to suggest that there have been no cosmologists who, misled by idealist epistemologies, have not tried to turn the anthropic principle inside out. It is, however, one thing to pour idealism, Kantian, even Berkelian, into scientific cosmology; it is another to face the cosmic facts in their enormous singularity and specificity. If anything is singular, that is, specific, the primordial mix of the universe is certainly such. That mix, as described above in simple quantitative terms, is primordial only in a provisional sense. Cosmologists have already reduced that mix to even more primordial states that existed only for fractions of a second. To describe those states, called lepton, hadron, and quantum states,[35] would involve too many technical steps. To those able to follow such steps the emerging picture would appear no less startlingly specific. The view of such specificity, cutting through the cosmos from its very core to its farthest reaches, should discourage any thought that such specificity is the reflection of a priori categories of the mind. Only queer minds would ever think that reality is not specific to the point of being queer.

The specificity of the universe discussed here is a quantitative feature. It is not the deepest aspect of the specificity of existence but a very telling one nonetheless. It tells nothing less than that man can take in a literal sense the measure of the universe. In doing so man proves not only that he is a conqueror of the universe, but also that he is not the measure of the universe. Contrary to Protagoras (at least as popularized), the size, the structure, the curvature, the quantity, and the timetable of the universe are not stamped by man on the universe. Man merely has the ability to find those specifications, so many wonders of the universe. By tracing out those cosmic wonders through the wonder which is science, man proves that he is the most wonderful thing in nature, in proof of Sophocles' dictum. Clearly, man, so much a part and parcel of the universe, is also superior to it. Man who knows the universe with a grasp and precision which is simply astonishing cannot be a mere beast, however advanced, whose universe is limited to the surroundings available to its sensory organs. The conceptual grasp by man of a universe, which is specific to the point of being queer, also forestalls the temptation that he should think of himself as an angel. The newly-emerged picture of the universe should indeed seem very humbling to those tempted to play the role of an angel. A proof of this is the stunned reaction of agnostic astronomers, if not plain atheists, who are visibly troubled by this new and wholly scientific vision of the cosmos.[36] It is a vision of a transparency beyond which shine the words: Let there be light.

A mirage dissipated

The light in question is very different from the one which a
Lucifer, a Descartes, a Kant, and other fallen angels wanted to bring
to man. That light was a mirage resulting from the deification of
Euclidean geometry, first by Descartes and then by Kant. Descartes
did so by ontologizing three-dimensional extension, which in the
hands of Kant became the framework of mind into which all sensory data had to be fitted. Kant was indeed the modern Procrustes
who, so the story goes, captured all travelers visiting in Attica and
stretched them until they completely covered a very long bed. He
also had a short bed for quicker and more drastic results. Any
traveler longer than that bed had a few inches chopped off his feet.
So much about the myth. The best amplification of it is due to Eddington according to whom Procrustes duly reported to the
Anthropological Society in Attica that he had obtained experimental verification concerning the identity of height of all travelers
through the region.[37]

Eddington wanted to lampoon the a priori method, the very
opposite of the experimental approach. Curiously, he did not realize
that he was implicating his own gigantic efforts to prove in an a
priori, almost Kantian way, that the universe can only be what it is,
because human thinking is what it is.[38] Nor did Eddington notice
the punchline of the myth of Procrustes. For his cruelty Procrustes
found his demise in the hands of Theseus, the god of the good old
earth, the primary symbol of material reality. The myth therefore is
also symbolic of the vengeance which good, old, down-to-earth,
material reality takes on any a priori fitting of facts to theories.
Descartes, Kant, and all other modern Procrustes, suffered their
defeat in the hands of such a symbolic Theseus, for their trying to
tailor the universe to the specifications of Euclidean geometry, or
rather to the exigencies of their misguided minds. As befitted willful
theorizers, they failed to notice the patent contradictoriness of an
infinite Euclidean universe. And so did many scientists to the end of
the 19th century, which, as already noted, witnessed the unabashed
surfacing of agnosticism and materialism in the Western world. The
reason for the naive and stubborn espousal of the infinite Euclidean
universe with its homogeneous distribution of stars rests ultimately
with the fact that such an infinite can, to the delight of agnostics and

materialists, readily play the role of a substitute for the true Infinite, or God. Such a substitute infinity is the choice playground for fallen angels as well as for glorified apes.

The chief trouble with that physical infinity in the Euclidean sense was its being a bastard product of the countermetaphysical cravings of man separated from God. Such an infinity could not be a consistent object for knowledge and it certainly could not be handled by science. The infinity in question was contradictory. It implied what science is most fearful of: the appearance in the equations of the sign ∞ which beckons catastrophe.[39] In this case the infinity took the form of an infinite gravitational potential at any point.[40] In such a universe no material entity can be imagined to exist. In a somewhat primitive way Richard Bentley had already called public attention to this contradictory character of an infinite Euclidean universe before Newton's century was out.[41] Curiously, Newton, who was alerted to this problem by Bentley in private letters, failed to perceive its significance. Nor was notice taken by scientists and philosophers in England, or in Germany (where Bentley's book was published in translation in 1711). The attitude was well exemplified by Halley who, in discussing in 1721 the optical counterpart of the paradox, found it of no real significance. When a hundred years later the same optical paradox of the darkness of the night sky was discussed by Olbers, it was clear that belief in Euclidean infinity was so strong as to prevent proper weighing of objections to it. Olbers, in fact, started with a reference to Kant as an authority above any appeal concerning the infinity of space and universe. This certainly showed the ease with which the contradictoriness of the teaching of a philosopher is perpetuated on no other ground except his presumed excellence. While Kant claimed on the one hand that space represented the antinomy between infinite and finite, on the other he held Euclidean space to be a category of the mind. This contradiction Kant never resolved.

Curiously, Bernhard Riemann made no reference to Kant in his famous 1854 lecture on the application of non-Euclidean geometry to physical space and advocated its finiteness. It may of course be that Kant was the target of Riemann's concluding remark about traditional prejudices which check "progress in the knowledge of the interdependence of things."[42] Again Kant was not

mentioned when, in 1871, Zöllner showed, more than fifty years
before Einstein, that Riemann's paper provided a satisfactory solution to the gravitational paradox of an infinite homogeneous universe. The solution was, however, drastic. The total mass con-
stituting the universe had to be imagined to be strictly finite,
producing a closed four-dimensional space.[43] Kant was not,
however, left unmentioned when, two years later, the mathematician Clifford discussed before the Royal Institution the importance
of Riemann's work. Clifford's starting point was Spencerian
evolutionism in which the parameters of the human mind were seen
to be the fruits of sense perception that slowly accumulated from
the lowest animals to man. Since none of these ever could experience infinity, its Kantian doctrine as an a priori truth was in obvious jeopardy. Riemann's great achievement, by postulating a
closed space, was, Clifford argued, nothing less than that "in this
case the universe, as known, becomes again a valid conception."[44]

Fatal blows at apriorism

This was a point whose significance for the construction of an
objectivist and metaphysical theory of human knowledge Clifford
failed to perceive. Unlike Mill, who argued somewhat earlier that
material reality which empiricism provided was merely "the permanent possibility of sensations"[45] —a perfectly satisfactory state of
affairs for a beast however glorified—Clifford did not realize that
objective cosmology has always been the citadel of theists.[46] At any
rate, any departure from Euclidean geometry as cosmological
framework rings the deathknell for Kant's subjectivist cosmology
and anthropology. That the construction of non-Euclidean
geometries struck a blow at Kant's epistemology was noted a
hundred years ago by Helmholtz.[47] The mind can do much more
than Kant imagined. Nor is the mind limited to the sensory which in
no way can be seen as the source of non-Euclidean geometries and
of an increasing number of mathematical systems which deliberately disregard the physical world.[48] Yet, whatever his wizardry with a
mathematics wholly separated from empirical realities, man is not
an angel. He is unable to explain why some of those mathematical
theories (such as group theory or non-commutative algebra, to
mention only two examples) turn out to be astonishingly useful for

physical theory.[49] Not being an angel, man cannot dictate to nature, but being much more than an ape man is able to probe nature throughout and prove thereby that he is superior to it.

To probe nature means to test our ideas against facts, all of which appear the more peculiar the closer we look at them. The peculiarity, or queerness of things, of everything, will impress only those who still have something of the philosophical ability to wonder, a commodity in short supply in an age of science. The responsibility for this lies not so much with science as with the popularity of its shallow interpretations. A closer look at science shows it to be steeped in philosophy and wonderment. Those unwilling to take a deeper breath than what is needed for exercises in logic and mathematics have no right to ignore the fact, convincingly demonstrated by Gödel's theorems of incompleteness, that neither mathematics nor logic can have its foundations within itself.[50] Insofar as Gödel's finding is true, and it has stood every test since its formulation half-a-century ago, it is also true that a rigorous axiomatization of mathematics and logic is impossible. Both fields are inevitably incomplete, insofar as neither can have its ultimate foundation or justification within its own set of postulates. Ironically, Gödel formulated his theorems at a time when Hilbert's program of giving a definitive axiomatization to mathematics seemed to be on the verge of final success.[51] The damper which Gödel's conclusions have quickly become for better mathematicians was well expressed by H. Weyl. He spoke of Gödel's finding as a "constant drain on the enthusiasm" with which he pursued his work. Weyl could also be trusted concerning his conviction that his experience was shared by "other mathematicians who are not indifferent to what their scientific endeavors mean in the context of man's whole caring and knowing, suffering and creative existence in the world."[52] Clearly, Weyl and some others hoped to overcome the burdens of human existence by securing ultimate necessary truths at least in their mathematical form. That hope turned out to be a dream which could only drain a misguided enthusiasm.

What has been learned at least by the better mathematicians is still to be learned by not a few physicists working in the forefront of probing into the very foundations of nature. They still think—the statements of a Murray Gell-Mann, Weinberg, Hawking and others are a proof[53]—that it is possible to devise the ultimate, all-comprehensive physical theory. Such a theory not only would fit all known facts. It would not only assure us that facts to be detected in the future would fit the theory. It would also assure us that nature can contain no facts contrary to that theory. In other words, such a final theory would be a proof that nature is necessarily what it is and cannot be anything else. A nature, a universe, which would carry the label "necessary" would, of course, be in no need of a Creator. In fact, no reasoning could make God the Creator so unnecessary as such a final physical theory.

As one may guess it, behind such a lofty aim in physics there may lie motivations which are not at all so lofty. One could only wish that such physicists would be more explicit on the connection between their aims in physics and their avowed agnosticism, atheism, materialism, and perhaps sheer Freudianism. The fallen angel, which swayed a Descartes, and the glorified ape, which lured a Rousseau, can just as well be operative in the 20th century and in some of its most prominent physicists. The latter could have spared themselves such a possibility had they remembered Gödel's theorems and put two and two together.[54] Indeed the whole point is no less elementary than that. First, nothing is easier to grasp, even by an outsider to physics, than that any modern physical theory must be heavily mathematical. Therefore, in virtue of Gödel's theorems, the physical theory will, in its mathematical part, lack that consistency without which its finality cannot be guaranteed. That mathematical part is also largely the concpetual part of the physical theory. As to its other part, or the array of experimental data within its grasp, it should be exhaustive in its own right as long as the theory lays claim to finality.

Ideas and facts in wedlock

That there are some physicists, including an occasional Nobel Prize-winner, who claim, implicitly at least, that their theory covers all facts—past, present, and future—and do so without blushing,[55] calls at least for one comment. Ideas and facts constitute a pair of which one or the other can easily be neglected by sanguine individuals ready to claim to have conquered everything. In the position typified by Descartes facts went overboard. In the position exemplified by Rousseau, ideas were jettisoned. Yet ideas and facts prove time and again that they form a coherence within which they retain their distinctness which no solvent, however clever, can undo. Theirs is a wedlock which no man may put asunder without inviting disaster. Their indissoluble unity, coupled with their respective unsolubility, is as old as philosophy or science itself. Originality in this respect is possible only inasmuch as the old truth is recognized to be very valid in a new field of research. Jean Piaget will certainly be remembered for his pioneering work in the intellectual development of the child. Since the prehistoric dawn of intelligence will forever remain a closed book for research, the mental awakening of a child remains the only field where intelligence can be studied in its genesis. It is a new field largely opened up by Piaget. Like any good scientist, Piaget, too, went about his research by trying to demonstrate a theory by facts, without considering at first what he was really doing. By an instinct typical of a good scientist, Piaget did not try it the other way round, the Baconian empiricist way, gathering facts in order to have a theory. The facts to be gathered for science must be relevant facts and this shows that theory, or concepts, must be at least on a par with what the senses tell us.

The so-called equilibration of cognitive states, which served Piaget as his conceptual guide in looking at facts smacks, of course, of physicalism. It would have blindfolded any lesser scientist than Piaget. In the end he was even able to see the obvious, namely, that ideas were not identical with experimental data. In the Preface of one of his last works, *The Development of Thought: Equilibration of Cognitive Structures*, he admitted nothing less than that the physicalist model used in his magnum opus, *Studies in Genetic Epistemology*, proved to be insufficient. There he also stated that it was imperative to restudy the problem completely in view of the overriding importance of the genetic view of knowledge. Although obviously committed to the primacy of a materialistic evolutionary view, Piaget discovered something stable across the ever-changing landscape, something which in fact transcended a materialistic evolution: "The central idea is that knowledge proceeds neither solely from the experience of objects, nor from an innate programming performed in the subject, but from successive constructions, the result of the constant development of new structures."[56]

Such an admission is inexhaustible in philosophical significance. More than this ought not to be expected from a scientist steeped in physicalism and evolutionism,[57] two fields that have given too many evidences of their philosophical poverty. The admission shows how a great and honest scientist is driven in spite of himself to the recognition of the mutual irreducibility of facts and ideas. What a Christian will do with such an admission will largely depend on the measure to which he is not the victim of philosophical poverty. He is philosophically impoverished if he remembers only one half of Saint Paul: Paul rejecting the wisdom of the world lest the scandal of the cross of Christ become void of meaning.[58] No less an integral part of the Christian stance is evidenced by that same Paul who insisted that from the works of nature the Creator can and ought to be recognized.[59] Clearly, the Paul speaking of dead Christians as somehow still alive—they were merely asleep in the Lord[60]—must not be construed as playing with words. He would have done precisely this if survival of bodily death did not mean the actual existence of a soul, which is both a proposition of faith and a proposition accessible to reason.[61] Reason indeed can provide us with certainty about objects that cannot be seen, such as the soul and the universe—and God, to mention only the chief of such objects.[62] The certainty is of course to be distinguished carefully from the demonstrations of mathematics and geometry, all too often taken for exclusive roads to certainty. Instead of giving certainty they merely inform us about tautologies.

Such distinctions should help prevent us, as Christians, from separating faith from reason. Christians who make that fateful separation can only engage in losing battles while hoping to win the war—before eternity dawns on us all. But even those Christians who are not suspicious of reason may choose grounds where battles can only be lost. The age of the earth, the age of man, the origin of organic life and similar propositions, which can be proved or disproved empirically—because they are empirical propositions—are such slippery grounds. The uniqueness of man calls for selecting a ground where not only battles can be won, but also where the war can be carried on until the very moment when eternity does set in. Sustaining war efforts to the end is the most a Christian can look for in this existence of ours about which Scripture says that it is a kind of military service. This insight, it is well to recall, came to Job as he was losing battle after battle without ever despairing of the war's final outcome.[63] A final victory on earth would be conceivable only if philosophical sensitivity could become a commodity universally shared. Since we do not dwell in Utopia, but rather in a vale of tears,[64] philosophical sensitivity will remain rare, even among those who are supposed to be the children of wisdom and light. In the absence of that philosophical depth, which alone can give positive conviction about the uniqueness of man, a largely negative method is all one has left—although such method ought not be slighted. To use it to best advantage one has to be well-versed in logical skills which are far easier to learn than mastering philosophy. One has also to be well-informed about what is really going on in the opposite camp.

Those on the opposite side will keep striving to do the impossible, namely, to show that there is reason and consistency in presenting man as not essentially superior to the rest of nature. Such an effort inevitably bogs down in contradictions and blunders. Nowhere are these more visible than in statements, the like of which are a commonplace in evolutionary apotheoses of man: that he is the phase in which the cosmic process gains consciousness and begins to comprehend itself.[65] The blunder of the presentation lies in its anthropomorphism. It presents Nature as a personality with striving, a procedure which flies in the face of that very resolve that helped science rise four hundred years ago. The resolve was aimed at avoiding all considerations of purpose and consciousness when it came to the processes of nature. In reply, protagonists of evolutionary philosophy note that a figure of speech, which personifies Nature, must not be taken seriously. Undoubtedly not, but only if it is a slip of the tongue and not a device continually relied upon. Systematic reliance on "unscientific" style proves the impossibility of speaking of an unconscious evolution which issues in consciousness without relying upon words and phrases implying consciousness and purpose. Those words and phrases are either meant or they are not meant. If they are meant, the blunder is coupled with begging the question. If they are not meant, the trick of speaking from both corners of the mouth is being played, a performance worse than a blunder.

Such chinks if not plain rusting in the enemy's armor can be spotted by any eye sensitive to the contours of logic. More than logic, thorough factual information about the opposite camp is required for spotting its penchant for beating retreat at regular intervals, a priceless evidence of man's unconquerability. A survey of the mental odyssey of the leaders of that crusading camp would be no less telling than the intellectual itinerary of Descartes and Rousseau who shed unintended light on the fate and fortune of man as a fallen angel and on his physiognomy as a glorified ape. The most powerful portrayal of man's unconquerability was not, however, provided by anyone in those camps. Not that Einstein ever held that man was unconquerable. Yet he became an unwitting, though most persuasive, witness of man's unconquerability by contributing more than any other scientist to that consistent scientific cosmology which expresses man's conquest of the universe. A look at Einstein's scientific quest and at the spirited stance he took with respect to the true nature of his conquest retain an instructiveness worth many a formal argument.

Einstein's quest

The philosophy imbibed by young Einstein hardly predisposed him to a quest aimed at the conquest of the universe. Cosmology, or the reasoned grasp of the universe, had neither appeal nor validity for an admirer of Mach, which young Einstein professed himself to be. While his theory of general relativity was nearing completion (around 1916), Einstein could not have been unaware of Mach's thoroughgoing sensationism; nevertheless he still failed to see the wide gap between the precept which he had followed, however tacitly, and the precepts legislated by Mach for physics. Chief among Mach's precepts was that only what is directly observable, that is, a datum of the sensory, can enter into physical theory. In a superficial sense Einstein's special theory of relativity obeyed that precept. That theory is usually remembered as dealing a death-blow to the ether, a postulated "entity" about which a series of sophisticated experiments could not obtain sensory evidence. Einstein himself must have seen his work in this light when he eulogized Mach in 1916 as the one who, half-a-century earlier, could very well have formulated relativity theory. Years later, however, Einstein flatly stated that even if he did use Mach's method, that method was non-sense nonetheless.[67]

At any rate, Einstein could easily concede to Mach the possibility of formulating special relativity because Poincaré, Lorentz and others did in fact formulate it almost in full just in the years preceding the publication in 1905 of Einstein's famous paper on it.[68] Einstein, of course, was always fully aware of the originality of his work on general relativity. Yet, even with respect to special relativity, he surmised aspects of his thinking which put him in a camp very different from sensationism, which invariably invites philosophical relativism. Thus in 1921 he deplored, in private at least, that his theory had become known as "relativity theory" and not as invariance theory.[69] The equivalence of all inertial reference systems, the relativity of all motion with respect to the observer, the impossibility of measuring the simultaneity of events taking place at different points, formed only the surface of special relativity. Beneath the surface lay Einstein's conviction, hardly explainable by Mach's sensationism, that the laws of physics (Maxwell's electromagnetic equations, to be specific) carried a validity and beauty in their very from which was to be retained regardless of the reference system to which they were related. The price to be paid for such an "ontological" conviction was nothing less than the recognition of the absolute, though not directly and in its ultimate form, which is God. Yet the postulate that the speed of light must have a constant value which is independent of the observer, of the velocity of its source, even of its reference system, was a step toward the absolute.[70] This step further revealed its true nature with the extension of the procedure to accelerated reference systems, mainly exemplified by gravitational fields. Coupled with the reliance on non-Euclidean geometries, this step made consistent scientific cosmology possible, and through it the conquest of the universe. The absolutist or rather realist character of Einstein's relativity could not fail to assert itself anew: The over-all curvature of space-time generated by the total mass of the universe and in particular its expansion, to say nothing of the cosmic background radiation, could in no way be considered as a relative framework.[71] This also implied the recognition that physical existence was not a product of the mind, though in its metric aspects fully explorable and con-

querable by the mind. The mind therefore could not be the product
of mere matter unless matter were equated with intelligence, and
intelligence were a mere reflection of matter. Whatever the
philosophical merits of such an equation, it certainly empties the act
of scientific discovery of its very nature.

This is not to suggest that Einstein had drawn a metaphysical
conclusion about the existence of a mind different from matter. But
something akin to the recognition that man the scientist was more
than mere matter was in order if it was true that Mach's sensationism could be useful for compiling catalogues but useless for
the quest which is the science of physics. When Einstein stated this
at the Sorbonne in 1922 before an almost disbelieving audience of
leading scientists and philosophers,[72] he reached the watershed of a
journey which he began as a sensationist and ended as a true realist
who is always a metaphysician. Such a consistent adept of Mach's
sensationism as Philipp Frank sensed unerringly that metaphysics
was raising its spectre when, in 1929, he heard from a well-known
German physicist that Einstein came around to Planck's view, according to which physical laws describe a reality in space and time
as independent of ourselves.[73] A year later, Einstein told Moritz
Schlick, leader of the Vienna Circle, that such was indeed the case.
Einstein's letter to Schlick was signed "the metaphysician
Einstein," and contained not only a disavowal of the positivist interpretation of physics but also the phrase that "every . . . two-
legged animal is de facto . . . a metaphysician."[74] To Schlick the
implication of this could not remain hidden. If there was an animal
which could do metaphysics and not be at the same time the victim
of mere illusion, such an animal had to be endowed with a mind that
transcended the physical.

The conqueror's stance

To be sure, Einstein did not believe in the soul's immortality.
He believed, however, in the existence of external reality in a way
that implied the existence of a mind that was more than mere matter. Einstein's often-quoted statement, "Belief in an external world,
independent of the perceiving subject, is the basis of all natural
science," may sound trivial in itself. Seven years later, in 1938, a
similar statement formed the grand conclusion of *The Evolution of*

Physics which Einstein wrote in collaboration with L. Infeld.[76] Far from being trivial, those statements contained the very essence of the stance which Einstein took publicly in the 1930s, on his achievements in physics. He staunchly defended that stance for the rest of his life, although he saw himself more and more isolated from fellow physicists and from philosophers who staked their message on their interpretation of physics. The stance was unabashedly and fearlessly metaphysical. Towering figure though Bertrand Russell was, Einstein was not afraid to spot in Russell's theory of knowledge "the fateful fear of metaphysics . . . which has become a malady of contemporary empiricist philosophy."[77] Nor was Einstein embarrassed to separate himself from the positivist camp even though he was thereby to incur their charge that he was, to quote his words, "guilty of the original sin of metaphysics."[78]

His major confrontation was, of course, with fellow physicists who, almost to a man, advocated the statistical interpretation of quantum mechanics and of reality itself. The story has often been told, though almost invariably in a way which fails to convey the essence of the conflict. Einstein's staunch defense of strict causality was as little the ultimate bedrock of his philosophy as was the absence of causality at the atomic level the fundamental tenet of the Copenhagen school, whose chief spokesman was Niels Bohr, Einstein's leading antagonist. Einstein was lured to a field where only the less-fundamental issue could be fought, and where he could only lose the battle.[79] For as long as a physicist had to rely on waves and quanta, his measurement (actual or idealized) of the physical processes could not be absolutely precise. Curiously, Einstein failed to see that absence of absolute precision in measurement was a very different proposition from the absence of strict causality in the physical interaction itself. Failure to see that elementary logic was no less curious on the part of Einstein's opponents. Clearly, much more than logic was implicit in the clash, as evidenced by the sundry dicta of Bohr and his disciples. Causality could easily by sacrificed when the sense of reality had already been victimized by that subjectivism which is inevitably generated by pragmatism, positivism, and idealism, all variations of the philosophy to which members of the Copenhagen school subscribed. Though Einstein was able to free himself, after years of groping,[80] from the shackles of philosophical subjectivism, most of his fellow physicists could not. Unfortunately, it was only after Einstein's death that some of his most penetrating (and most acid) reflections on his opponents' inability were made public. He felt, as he put it in 1950 in a letter to Schrödinger, that the Copenhagen people did not realize "what a dangerous game they were playing with reality."[81] The name of the game was best expressed by Einstein's one-line summary of Bohr's interpretation of quantum mechanics which, he says, admits, "no reality independent of the *probable subject*" (italics added).[82]

The penetrating force of that phrase makes learned volumes on the philosophy of quantum mechanics pale into insignificance. As Einstein correctly saw, the lack of sensitivity toward external reality turned even the reality of the subject into a mere probability. (This was not, of course, true for solipsists, but they must forever renounce the possibility of communication). Unfortunately, Einstein was not the articulate philosopher who would see the epistemological priority of reality over causality. He merely hung on to both with an elemental instinct and conviction. Even less of a philosopher was Pauli, who, perceiving that the ultimate issue between Einstein and the Copenhagen school was not so much causality as the status of external reality, brushed the matter off by carrying on with that dangerous game. In calling Max Born's attention to the real bone of contention between him and Einstein, Pauli characterized the ultimate issue with the remark that "one should no more rack one's brain about the problem of whether something one *cannot know* anything about *exists* all the same, than about the ancient question of how many angels are able to sit on the point of a needle" (italics added).[82]

A remark which suddenly conjured up medieval philosophers was far more appropriate than Pauli suspected. Whatever their alleged interest in angels on pinheads, medieval philosophers had external reality for their chief concern, and they never advocated the patently fallacious claim that a reality that could not be measured exactly could not exist. Reality was known by what is nowadays referred to as commonsense perception, something much more than mere measurement. This was a basic tenet with Aquinas and with all disciples of Aristotle. Einstein unwittingly echoed them as he made his most valid epistemological comment: "The whole of science is nothing more than a refinement of everyday thinking. It is for this reason that the critical thinking of the physicist cannot possibly be restricted to the examination of the concepts of his own specific field. He cannot proceed without considering critically a much more difficult problem, the problem of analyzing the nature of everyday thinking."[83]

Once the primacy of everyday knowledge is granted, the idealist position, be it Kantian criticism, which underlies the Copenhagen interpretation of quantum mechanics, loses its foundation. At any rate, Kantian idealism rests on circularity in reasoning. Criticism of knowledge as advocated by Kant cannot be the first step in knowledge because criticism is meaningful only if it is the knowledge of something. As to Bohr and his cohorts, they could have learned from the idealist Eddington that ultimately all physics is "non-atomic" or molar, because the pointer needles of the observer and the observer himself are molar, that is, the object of commonsense perception.[85]

The primacy of commonsense knowledge, the unconquerable basis of realism and metaphysics (and even of criticism of any sort), is also the only avenue leading to the true nature of man. It is also the tool of man's conquest of the universe. For it is commonsense, or direct, immediate knowledge of external reality (a knowledge to be distinguished from "common sense," which is a subtle relapse into Cartesian innatism,[86] and all too fallible for that matter), which assures man of the orderliness of nature, the very basis of the consistency of human knowledge. It is man's continual reliance on that immediate direct knowledge of reality which enables him to correct and criticize any knowledge, and which also gives him confidence that even that reality is orderly which he cannot yet perceive and explore. Such is the basic presupposition without which science cannot exist. As Einstein realized, there is no a priori reason to assume that there is a high degree of orderliness in physical reality. Insofar, Einstein concluded, as such order was ascertained by science, it was a miracle.[87]

Clearly, Einstein could not deny his sensationist beginnings. As an erstwhile sensationist he could not see that knowledge of reality was the perception of the intelligible in the sensory. To a sensationist, the unpredictable orderliness of the world, the chief evidence of its intelligibility, which turned out to be very different from a simplistic three-dimensional framework of sensations, could but appear a miracle, that is, an unexplainable fact. He was quick to add that in no way should a God be seen behind that miracle as its explanation.[88] With a less biased philosophical preconditioning, Einstein may have rather spoken of wonderment. For knowledge is ever fresh wonder, and yet very natural to an unspoiled mind. To know is man's nature and not a magic to dazzle him. Knowledge, when it becomes magic, ends in a celebration of unintelligibility in the name of understanding equated either with apriorism or with sensationism. Einstein relapsed into sensationism as he declared that "the very fact that the totality of our sense experiences is such that by means of thinking . . . it can be put in order . . . is a fact which leaves us in awe but which we shall never understand."[89] Pulled by his erstwhile sensationism, Einstein could not help being overly impressed by the power of knowledge. He also served evidence that any extreme invites its opposite. In his case, sensationism propelled him into apriorism. Time and again he spoke as if his reflections could prescribe the true form of the universe. On being asked what would have been his reaction had the eclipse observation in 1919 not shown the bending of light, he quipped: "I would have been very sorry for the dear Lord—the theory is correct."[90] His unified field theory was to be such, he felt, that even the good Lord could not have done it any better, let alone differently. His ultimate interest in science, he said, was to know "whether God had any choice in the creation of the world."[91]

Einstein might have become another Descartes, a "fallen angel," had it not been for his scientific instinct. It prevented him from losing sight of the fact that the ultimate truth of any theory, however superb, rested with experimental verification. About the same time he was tempted to feel sorry for the dear Lord, he stated to *The* [London] *Times*: "If a single one of the conclusions drawn from it [General Relativity] proves wrong, it must be given up; to modify it without destroying the whole structure seems to be impossible."[92] A year later, in 1920, he told a vast audience that one single experiment could turn his General Relativity "into mere dust and ashes."[93] Instinctive, scientific respect for the good old earth, or material reality, kept Einstein's feet on the ground. That the same ground could prove for him an assurance for views soaring far above it, nay above all matter, was another matter and a very metaphysical one at that.

Farce and tragedy

All this expressed in a new key the old tune that man was both matter and mind. That evolutionists for the most part fail to face up to this conclusion is in no small part due to the fact that in thinking about science they still think in terms of a long-outdated mechanistic physics. To be sure, a close look at the best in mechanistic physics would show the indispensable interplay between mind and experience and show both to be mutually irreducible. Physics, as fashioned by Einstein, is a far more powerful pointer in this respect, although a pointer more difficult to read than was the case with mechanistic physics. Were it to be read by Darwinists, they would think twice before carrying their logic as far as to debase the history of scientific thought into a struggle for survival among competing ideas and theories as if they were so many small animals.[94] This debasement is tantamount to sinking in the morass of an all-pervasive flux in which progress is impossible because nothing can be permanent. What is usually bemoaned concerning such an outcome is the vanishing of progress even in science, that most persuasive assurance of the reality of progress. But the most serious aspect of this Darwinistic interpretation of scientific thinking lies in its blissful advocacy of an elementary fallacy, a chief characteristic of Darwinian philosophising. The proposition of a universal flux is fallacious on the basis of both realism and idealism. If the flux is an imposition on reality of a category of mind, then at least that category is not subject to that flux. If the flux is a reality, then it cannot elicit on man's part a knowledge of it which is exempt from radical fluctuation.

The Darwinian interpretation of knowledge in general and of science in particular has, in the fallaciousness of its reasoning, elements of farce; it has also elements of tragedy. Man's repeated and ever more threatening misuses of his scientific tools will appear as the blind outpacing of man's instincts by man's science.[95] Not being a systematic thinker, Rousseau could not foresee this development, but would see his distrust of science justified by it. We in the 20th century are not allowed to savor such gratification. To cope with that runaway prospect a genetic retooling of the whole of mankind may seem the answer. The question remains: Who will manipulate those who claim to themselves the role of manipulating the rest? As to those Darwinists (biologists, anthropologists, sociologists, psychologists, and philosophers) who merely want to continue their clever though superficial game with man, they would do well to reflect on the proverb: "If you wish to drown, do not torture yourself [and your fellow men] with shallow waters."[96]

The proverb may stand in good stead also Christians who want a "definite" proof on behalf of their conviction that there is in man something specially created by God. Unfortunately, they want more than the only definitive answer to be had, the answer of perennial philosophy which is methodical realism. Worse, all too often they do not even want to hear the voice of that philosophy. No wonder that they look askance at a skull, a jawbone, a rock, or what not, so many ominous reminders of lost innocence. In their longing for innocence they all too readily put and answer the problem as Disraeli did when the Darwinian dispute reached its first peak: "What is the question now placed before society with a glib assurance the most astounding? The question is this—Is man an ape or an angel? My Lord, I am on the side of the angels." Of course, by angels Disraeli meant to say men. He had just identified the highest science as the one which interprets man, "the highest nature."[97] Still, the fact that his tongue so readily slipped from men to angels was symbolic. All too often Christians oppose the shallows of materialistic reductionism with its spiritualistic equivalent. The latter may perhaps lead to the realm of angels, but gives no access to the species, homo sapiens, which is certainly inaccessible to Darwinism.

Unconquerable man

Imbued with that perennial philosophy and with enduring realism, Christians would not only gain a firm hold on man—and themselves—but they would also be able to take immense comfort from the fact that reductionism is caught in an ever recurring pattern of circularity, particularly evident in its Darwinian version. The irreducibility of man, either to mind, or to body, remains intact under any assault of reductionism, idealist or materialist. But because man is a mysterious unity of mind and matter, his witness will be similar to a tug of war, now going in the direction of his mind, now in the direction of his body. The tug of war, and this is the all-important point to note, keeps going on because man is neither an angel nor an ape. That this tug of war has outlasted those—a Descartes, a Kant, a Rousseau, a Darwin—who believed they had put an end to it, and that behaviorists and sociobiologists are no match for it, should suggest that man is unconquerable. No wonder. Unlike an angel who needs no conquests, and unlike an ape uninterested in them, man thrives on conquests which are the fruit of a mysterious union in him of matter and mind.

Once this is ignored by man, he will be conquered not from without but from within. Then he will have no choice but to declare: "The more the universe seems comprehensible, the more it also seems pointless."[98] These words, coming as they do from a prominent cosmologist, prove all too well that man's finest conquest—his scientific grasp of the universe—will be self-defeating unless he is able to see the point of things, and especially of their totality, the universe. To do so, he must see the point of being himself. Only then will he not appear to himself a complex though hap-hazard agglomerate of matter but a complexity unified by purpose embodied in his mind, which is not, in the ultimate analysis, at the mercy of blind matter. Such an analysis will be successful only if anchored in the ultimate of intelligibility, which is God. Only with God in view will man be protected from ending up either as a fallen angel or a glorified ape and will his confidence, his most cherished possession, be protected from being sapped by his spectacular conquests, which ought to be so many proofs that he is unconquerable.

"If he exalt himself, I humble him; if he humble himself, I exalt him; and I always contradict him, till he understands that he is an incomprehensible monster."

—*Pascal*, Pensées *No. 420*

NOTES

Chapter One

1. No reference to Burman, or to his conversation with Descartes, is given in G. Cohen's *Ecrivains francais en Hollande dans la première moitié du XVIIᵉ siècle* (Paris: E. Champion, 1920), still the standard work on Descartes' sojourn of many years in the Netherlands. The actual place of the conversation must have been Egmond-binnen, a dependence of Egmond, where Descartes resided in a manor house from 1644 on. The account of the conversation in Descartes' massive biography by C. Adam, *La vie de Descartes*, which forms volume 12 in *Oeuvres de Descartes*, edited by C. Adam and P. Tannery (Paris: L. Cerf, 1897–1913), merely aims at showing that Descartes generously put himself at the service of inquiring youth (see pp. 483–84). More informative there is the remark that a friendly rapport existed between Descartes and Burman's father, a Protestant minister and a refugee in Holland from the Palatinate, an area particularly ravaged by the Thirty-Year War. The visit of young Burman, who in 1664 became professor of theology in Utrecht, must be seen against Calvinist attacks, led by Voetius, on Descartes who was charged, tellingly enough, with atheism. For a resumé of Burman's life and a list of his publications, see A. J. Van der AA, *Biographisch Woordenboek der Nederlanden* (new ed.; Tweede Deel—Vierde Stuk; Haarlem: J. J. van Brederode, n.d.), pp. 1592–94.

2. The printed text of their conversation in Latin covers more than thirty pages in *Oeuvres de Descartes*, 5:144–79.

3. Quoted in the translation of E. S. Haldane and G. R. T. Ross, *The Philosophical Works of Descartes* (Cambridge: University Press, 1931), 1:164.

4. Translated from the Latin, in *Oeuvres de Descartes,* 5:157.

5. Descartes was neither the first nor the last practicing Catholic whose philosophy was irreconcilable with his faith. It is hardly philosophical to take lightly, as was done by A. Kenny in his *Descartes: A Study of his Philosophy* (New York: Random House, 1968) the facts of Descartes' attachment to Catholic faith in order to resolve that contradiction. A mere reference to schizophrenia, all too evident in many a genius, would have been a greater help in understanding how

that faith could co-exist with a philosophy, which, as has been widely admitted for a long time, invited materialism.

6. Translated from *Dr. Martin Luther Sämmtliche Schriften*, edited by J. G. Walch, *Band 22. Colloquia oder Tischreden* (St. Louis: Lutherischer Concordia Verlag. 1887), p. 697.

7. *Institutes of the Christian Religion*, translated by F. L. Battles (The Library of Christian Classics, Volume XX—Philadelphia: Westminster Press, 1960), p. 166.

8. In what sense that catechism served on this point as a pattern for regional catechisms is well illustrated by the statement, "it is a matter of faith that God the creator produced out of nothing creatures both spiritual and corporal, angelic and earthly," in *A Catechism of Christian Doctrine. Revised edition of the Baltimore Catechism. A Text for Secondary Schools and Colleges* (Patterson, N.J.: St. Anthony Guild Press, 1952, p. 30) with a reference to the Fourth Lateran (1214) and First Vatican (1870) Councils.

9. One example may not be amiss. Not that A. J. Wilhelm, author of a widely used catechism for adults, *Christ Among Us: A Modern Presentation of the Catholic Faith* (2d rev. ed.: New York: Paulist Press, 1973) would simply dismiss angels and devils as purely mythological beings. The witness on behalf of their reality is too obvious in liturgical worship. But he certainly casts a clever doubt on their existence by the caption that "today, theology is restudying the whole question of angels and devils," and by the suggestion, "perhaps scripture simply presupposes angels and devils as part of the biblical milieu, rather than directly affirming their actual existence as part of God's revelation." Wilhelm's claim, "nor does the existence of angels and devils seem to be a part of the strictly dogmatic teaching of the Church" (p. 27), is an obvious slighting of the meaning of *dogmatic* and flies in the face of many a dogmatic utterance of the Church.

10. *The Peasant of the Garonne: An Old Layman Questions Himself about the Present Time*, translated by M. Cuddihy and E. Hughes (New York: Holt, Rinehart and Winston, 1968), pp. 6 and 55.

11. The eve of the feast of Saint Martin was a time of great merrymaking with Frenchmen long before Descartes and some time after. Hence his insistance that he had not tasted wine for days. He clearly did not want the suspicion arise that an all too ordinary cause may have triggered his dreams. He saw nothing suspicious in the steady rise of a warm pressure in his head for several days prior to the event. The dreams spoke for themselves. In the first Descartes sees himself buffeted by whirlwinds, in the second he imagines a thunderclap wakes him up and makes him see sparkles all around his room. He has peace only during the third dream, in which he sees a book of poems. On opening it he sees an unknown person give him another poem which begins with the dialectic "Est et Non." In the concluding part of that dream he sees himself pondering whether he was awake or still asleep. See Descartes' autobiographical fragments, "Olympica" preserved in A. Baillet's translation, in *Oeuvres de Descartes*, 10:181–82.

12. For details, see W. R. Shea, "Descartes and the Rosicrucians," in *Annali dell'Istituto e Museo di Storia della Scienza di Firenze* 4 (1979) :29–47.

13. See my introduction to my translation with notes of Bruno's *The Ash Wednesday Supper (La cena de le ceneri)* (The Hague: Mouton, 1975). The much broader aspects of Bruno's obscurantism are magisterially treated in *Giordano Bruno and the Hermetic Tradition* by F. Yates (Chicago: University of Chicago Press, 1964).

14. *Oeuvres de Descartes*, 10:213. While traveling, Descartes often acted as if he had to hide himself. On commenting on his resolve, following Galileo's condemnation, not to publish his *Le Monde*, Descartes noted in his letter of April 1634 to Father Mersenne: *bene vixit, bene qui latuit* (*Oeuvres*, 1:286).

15. This point was made emphatically by Jacques Maritain in his *Three Reformers: Luther—Descartes—Rousseau* (New York: Charles Scribner's Sons, 1929), p. 57.

16. The seven articles in qu. 58 of Part I of the *Summa theologiae* are devoted to the assertions that angelic intellect is not a potentiality, that it knows not discursively or by comparing and dividing, but simultaneously, and is never in error, owing to its access to innate ideas.

17. While for us moderns the nature of intuitive knowledge is beclouded by the role of imagination, with Descartes it was "the undoubting conception of an unclouded and attentive mind," unfettered by the "blundering constructions of imagination." Truths known in this way, he added, were "far more numerous than many people think." See Rule III in his *Rules for the Direction of the Mind* in *The Philosophical Works of Descartes*, 1:7. In Meditation III he held that the notion of God's existence was just as innate in man as was the notion of oneself (ibid., p. 170). As to the independence of knowledge of things, the entire Cartesian cosmogony is an illustration. On such a basis all men should have enjoyed an errorless way of knowing, a problem which Descartes tried to resolve with a reference to the special status of those blessed with taste for geometry.

18. These protestations of Descartes in *Principes de la philosophie* (Partie III, ch. 1, 2, 45 and 47) were emptied of whatever persuasiveness they had by the declaration in the *Discourse on the Method* that the laws of nature as demonstrated by him are such that "even if God had created other worlds, He could not have created any in which these laws would fail to be observed." *Philosophical Works*, 1:108.

19. *Discourse on the Method*, Part VI, *Philosophical Works*, 1:123–24.

20. In his letter of January 1630 to the ailing Mersenne, Descartes referred to his efforts to work out a medicine "based on infallible demonstration" (*Oeuvres*, 1:105) by which he may have implied a means of warding off bodily death. Fifteen years later he still spoke "of the conservation of health as the principal aim of my studies all the time" (ibid., 4:329) and felt certain that, although he could not promise immortality, he could make human life equal to the age of patriarchs (ibid., 11:671). Three years later, however, in his conversation with Burman, he spoke of his puzzlement over the long life of men prior to the deluge as "something which defies philosophy" (ibid., 5:178).

21. The label has become almost compulsory even with those who tried to salvage Descartes long after fascination with him began to fade in his own country. See, for instance, *Traité de paix entre Descartes & Newton* by H. A. Paulian (Avignon: chez la Veuve Girard, 1763), 1:248.

22. Curiously, in his *The Ghost in the Machine* (New York: Macmillan, 1967), Koestler makes no reference to Descartes.

23. *The Tragic Sense of Life*, translated by J. E. Crawford (1921: Dover reprint, New York, 1954), p. 34.

24. *Philosophical Works*, 1:85. This is not to suggest that Descartes was a man without deep feelings. As a young boy he was overwhelmed by the appearance of a young girl. Almost forty years later, he gave her name, Françoise, to his own daughter. His emotional ties to his common-law wife of some ten years were very

strong. His constant search for peaceful life may, however, indicate that it was essentially sentiments that he wanted to avoid.

25. *The Passions of the Mind*, Art. XXX, in *Philosophical Works*, 1:345.

26. Ibid., Art. XXXI; 1:345.

27. Ibid.

28. As conclusively shown by Etienne Gilson in his *Index scolastico-cartésien* (Paris: F. Alcan, 1912) and *La liberté chez Descartes et la théologie* (Paris: F. Alcan, 1913).

29. *Pascal's Pensées*, translated by W. F. Trotter, with an introduction by T. S. Eliot (New York: E. P. Dutton, 1958), p. 23 (No. 77).

30. One indeed must be grateful to P. Davies for his candid remark in the context of his discussion of that "quantum-state" that "many physicists believe that quantum effects remove the existence of a creation altogether, thereby rendering the universe infinitely old." See his *The Runaway Universe* (New York: Harper and Row, 1978), p. 49.

31. As evinced, for instance, by the investigations of A. Koestler, *The Act of Creation* (London: Hutchinson, 1964) and *The Creative Process in Science and Medicine. Proceedings of the C. H. Boehringer Sohn Symposium held at Kronberg, Taunus, 16—17 May 1974*, edited by H.A. Krebs and J.H. Shelley (Amsterdam: Excerpta Medica, 1975).

32. See the English translation, *Father Malebranche's Treatise concerning the Search after Truth, the Whole Work Compleat*, by T. Taylor (Oxford: printed by L. Lichfield, 1694), 2:61.

33. Empiricists and logical positivists, for whom "thinking deep" must appear "unphilosophical", will have to do with such clues to Newton's genius as his confining himself, to recall the words of a contemporary observer, to a "small quantity of bread with a little sack and water," whenever he wanted "to quicken his faculties and fix his attention." See L. T. More, *Isaac Newton: A Biography* (New York: Charles Scribner's Sons, 1934), p. 44.

34. Descartes himself could not have written a more Cartesian passage than the one in Query 31, which appeared first in 1706 as Query 23 of the Latin translation of the English original: "The Organs of Sense are not for enabling the Soul to perceive the Species of Things in its Sensorium, but only for conveying them thither" (Opticks [New York: Dover, 1952], p. 403).

35. *Pascal's Pensées*, p. 99 (No. 358).

36. *An Essay concerning Human Understanding*, edited with notes by A. C. Fraser (New York: Dover, 1959), 2:193—94 (Bk. IV, ch. iii).

37. Reported by Jean-Theophile Desaguliers in his Preface to his *Course of Experimental Philosophy* (3d ed.; London: A. Millar, 1763), p. viii.

38. Lambert's formal instruction did not extend beyond the third grade of elementary school. For details on his instructing himself, see the introduction of my translation with notes of his *Cosmological Letters on the Arrangement of the World Edifice* (New York: Science History Publications, 1976).

39. Several minor, and largely worthless scientific essays of Kant preceded his cosmogonical work, *Allgemeine Naturgeschichte und Theorie des Himmels* (1755), on which the Swedish mathematician and astronomer, C. V. L. Charlier, served the most appropriate judgment in his Hitchcock Lectures given in 1924 at the University of California: "Evidently the author [of the *Allgemeine Naturgeschichte*] has not himself studied even the first sections of Newton's *Prin-*

cipia . . . I consider the *Naturgeschichte* of Kant unsuitable and even dangerous as inviting feeble minds and minds uninstructed in natural philosophy to vain and fruitless speculations." (*Publications of the Astronomical Society of the Pacific* 27 [1925]:63). For further details on the scientific incompetence of the author of *Allgemeine Naturgeschichte* see my introduction to my translation with notes of that work: *Universal Natural History and Theory of the Heavens* (Edinburgh: Scottish Academic Press, 1981). For evidences proving Hume's competence in the sciences to be a sheer myth, see my Gifford Lectures, *The Road of Science and the Ways to God* (Chicago: University of Chicago Press, 1978), pp. 102–03 and 369–70.

40. Galileo, *Dialogue concerning the Two Chief World Systems*, translated by S. Drake (Berkeley: University of California Press, 1962), p. 328. Utilitarianism, as the ultimate bedrock of an ethical behavior for which no strict justification can be given, is presented unequivocally in the conclusion of Hume's *An Inquiry concerning the Principles of Morals*: "I cannot, *at present*, be more assured of any truth which I learn from reasoning and argument, than that personal merit consists entirely in the usefulness or agreeableness of qualities to the person himself possessed of them, or to others who have any intercourse with him" (Library of Liberal Arts edition, Indianapolis: Bobbs-Merrill, 1957, p. 98). The context is all the more notable, because there Hume is taken aback by the contrast between a lack of consensus in matters of morality in spite of the benevolence infused into all human hearts (p. 92) and the subjection, as revealed by science, of heavenly bodies "to their proper laws" (p. 98). Hume failed to realize that his philosophy in no way assured validity to the recognition, scientific or not, of such laws. That in the same breath Hume credited science even with the reduction to calculation of "the infinite itself," only revealed the amateur in him in matters scientific.

41. Hume repeatedly emphasized this point: "What we call a mind, is nothing but a heap or collection of different perceptions . . . . " A thinking being was constituted by a "mass of perceptions." Mind was merely a word for the sole reality, the "successive perceptions." See *Treatise of Human Nature*, Bk. 1, Part IV, secs. 2 and 6.

42. A good example is the passage in V. Mehta's *Fly and the Fly-Bottle: Encounters with British Intellectuals* (Harmondsworth: Penguin, 1962), p.83: "Wittgenstein's earthquake hit the philosophers of the twentieth century as hard as David Hume's cyclone—which swept away cause and effect from the human experience—had hit their eighteenth-century predecessors." Clearly then the cyclone itself was an exception to the universal nullity of cause-effect relationship.

43. See his Essay "Of the Rise and Progress of the Arts and Sciences," by far the longest of all the essays, in which he does his best to make it appear that a genius is merely the result of properly available sensations and therefore "runs along the earth." See *Essays, Moral, Political, and Literary* edited by T. H. Green and T. H. Grose (London: Longmans, Green and Co., 1898), 1:174–97.

44. As will be discussed in Chapter 3.

45. The allusion is to the well-known concluding phrase of Hume's *An Enquiry concerning Human Understanding*.

46. "Enquiry concerning the Clarity of the Principles of Natural Theology and Ethics" (1763) in *Kant: Selected Pre-Critical Writings and Correspondence*, translated and introduced by G. B. Kerferd and D. E. Walford, with a contribution by P. G. Lucas (Manchester: University Press, 1968), pp. 5–35; see especially p. 17.

47. "Bemerkungen zu den Beobachtungen über das Gefühl des Schönen und Erhabenen," in *Kant's gesammelte Schriften* (Berlin: Walter de Gruyter, 1901—), 20:45. This edition, sponsored by the Prussian Akademie der Wissenschaften, of Kant's writings will be referred to as AA.

48. Especially in Section 7 of Part 2 and in Part 3.

49. AA 9:25.

50. He did so in Part Three of his cosmogony (*Allgemeine Naturgeschichte*) where he speculated with great confidence on the moral and intellectual characteristics of the denizens of each planet of the solar system. The basis of his speculations was twofold. First, he argued that the density of matter greatly decreased from Mercury to Saturn. Second, he claimed that the intellectual parts of the respective planetary denizens were a function of the density of matter. He therefore pictured the denizens of Mercury as beings with exceedingly low intellectual capacity, whereas the denizens of Jupiter and especially of Saturn were depicted by him as superior geniuses. Compared with them our Newton was a mere ape. Such a conditioning of intellectual capacity by the density of matter was just a short step from attributing to matter the ability to think.

51. *Anthropology from a Pragmatic Point of View*, translated with an introduction and notes by M. J. Gregor (The Hague: Nijhoff, 1974), p. 96.

52. Ibid., p. 97.

53. *Julie* (VI, 8) in *Oeuvres complètes de Jean Jacques Rousseau* (Paris: Bibliothèque de la Pléiade, 1964), 2:693.

54. "Bemerkungen . . . " AA 20:46. A little later Kant remarked: "The quarters of women are closer to nature" (p. 50).

55. Ibid., p. 43. The basic inadequacy of the hallowed academic cliché in which Kant essentially appears as a reaction to Hume can easily be sensed by a perusal of the almost 200 pages of the "Bemerkungen", jotted down between 1763 and 1766, where the two dominant themes are metaphysics and Rousseau!

56. Ibid., pp. 58—59.

57. Ibid., p. 44.

58. Ibid., p. 181.

59. AA 10:143.

60. AA 18:69. As stated in those notes "the origin of the critical philosophy is found in the moral responsibility of action." F. Paulsen, who quotes this passage in his *Immanuel Kant: His Life and Doctrine* (tr. J. E. Creighton and A. Lefevre; New York: Charles Scribner's Sons, 1902, p. 96), is an example of Kant scholars who fail to see its significance, because they are unwilling to consider Rousseau's decisive impact on Kant on account of its patently "un-intellectual" character.

61. *La science allemande* (Paris: Hermann, 1915), pp. 17—18. As to the *Critique of Practical Reason*, it was, according to Duhem's pregnant remark, a similar commentary on the continuation of Pascal's dictum: "We have an idea of truth, invincible to all scepticism."

62. *Rousseau—Kant—Goethe*, translated by J. Gutman, P. O. Kristeller and J. H. Randall, Jr. (Princeton: University Press, 1945), p. 20.

63. "Bemerkungen . . . " AA 20:30.

64. *Kant's Opus postumum*, edited by A. Buchenau (Berlin: Walter de Gruyter, 1938), 1:145.

65. *Kant on Education (Ueber Pädagogik)*, translated by A. Chruton with an introduction by A. C. A. Foley Rhus Davids (Boston: D. C. Heath, 1900), p. 113.

God indeed comes out rather poorly in that program, if He emerges at all. He will not appear necessary, if, following Kant's precept, "at first we must ascribe *everything* to Nature, and afterwards Nature herself to God" (italics added; ibid., p. 111).

67. This was conceded by no less an admirer of Kant and no less a diligent student of his writings on science than A. E. Adickes in his *Kant als Naturforscher* (Berlin: W. De Gruyter, 1925), 2:204.

68. *Universal Natural History and Theory of the Heavens* (see 39 above), pp. 87 and 113.

69. "Bemerkungen . . . " AA 20:47.

70. *Opus postumum*, 1:25.

71. *Perpetual Peace*, with an introduction by N. M. Butler (New York: Columbia University Press, 1932), p. 28.

72. F. Wiedmann, *Hegel: An Illustrated Biography*, translated from the German by J. Neugroschel (New York: Pegasus, 1968), p. 20.

73. Ibid., p. 56.

74. Ibid., pp. 55–56.

75. References to this work will be to the English translation of its parts concerning the natural sciences, published under the title, *Hegel's Philosophy of Nature*, 3 vols. (London: George Allen and Unwin; New York: Humanities Press, 1969). The translator, M. J. Petry, referred, through a vast array of notes, many of Hegel's dicta to contemporary scientific literature in the hope that those notes would demonstrate Hegel's reliability in matters scientific. No competent historian of science would be impressed by much of what is contained in those notes.

76. Georg Simon Ohm, for instance.

77. Those three editions appeared in 1817, 1827 and 1830.

78. *Hegel's Philosophy of Nature*, 3:213.

79. Ibid., 1:223. The negation of space constituted the point, or a "being-for-self."

80. Ibid., 1:229.

81. As admitted by Hegel himself; ibid., 1:235.

82. Ibid., 1:237.

83. Ibid., 1:242.

84. Ibid., 1:243. In the same breath Hegel also ascribed repulsion to the nature of matter on the ground that matter and resistance are inseparable.

85. Ibid., 1:252.

86. Ibid., 1:269. Resentment of some German academics against Newton had by then been an old story. A good example is in the review in 1753 by A. G. Kaestner, professor of mathematics in Göttingen, of Thomas Wright's book on the Milky Way, discussed in my contribution, "The Wronging of Wright," to the Yourgrau Festschrift (New York; Plenum Press, in press).

87. Ibid., 2:147–48. On Goethe's appreciation, see Wiedmann, *Hegel*, pp. 83–84.

88. For documentation, see my "Goethe and the Physicists," *American Journal of Physics*, 37 (1969) :195–203.

89. *Hegel's Philosophy of Nature*, 2:21.

90. Ibid., 2:149. In the same context, Hegel excoriated the "professionals" (Newtonian physicists) and spoke of "the barbarity of reflection one encounters in Newton."

91. Ibid., 2:30.

92. Ibid., 2:33–40. "The chemical elements," Hegel added, "exhibit no order whatever" (ibid., 2:35), a statement which, chronologically, stands at midpoint between Lavoisier and Mendeleev.

93. Ibid., 2:187.

94. Ibid., 2:170.

95. Ibid., 3:24.

96. *Wissenschaft der Logik*, in *Hegel's Werke* (Berlin: Duncker und Humblot, 1833), 3:35–36.

97. On the rigorous provenance of those statements, hailing military dictatorship, from Hegel's basic presuppositions, see Etienne Gilson, *The Unity of Philosophical Experience* (New York: Charles Scribner's Sons, 1938), pp. 246–47.

98. Hegel, *The Philosophy of History*, translated by J. Sibree (New York: Dover, 1956), p. 26.

99. Or grim resolve as put by Hegel himself: "A World-historical individual . . . is devoted to the One Aim, regardless of all else" (ibid., p. 32).

100. See *Concerning the History of Religion and Philosophy in Germany,*in *Heinrich Heine. Selected Works*, translated and edited by H. M. Mustard (New York: Vintage Books, 1973), pp. 417–18. Thus man as a super-angel or World-Spirit behaved exactly as his ancestor, the "noble savage" of Rousseau whom already Napoleon correctly saw as the chief creator of the French Revolution. H. Taine had this logic in mind when, on studying the comportment of French peasants and workers suddenly turned into revolutionary militia, he saw in them "all of a sudden spring forth the barbarian, and, still worse, the primitive animal, the grinning, sanguinary, wanton baboon, who chuckles while he slays, and gambols over the ruin he has accomplished." *The French Revolution*, translated by J. Durand (New York: Henry Holt, 1878–85), 1:53.

Chapter Two

1. *The Confessions of Jean-Jacques Rousseau*, tranlated with an introduction by J. M. Cohen (Harmondsworth: Penguin Books, 1954), p. 113.

2. The namesake is Jean-Baptiste Rousseau (1671–1741) who, in his letter of July 14, 1715 to Brossette, also wrote that "whatever poetry borrows from mathematics makes the spirit arid and accustoms it to a material ideal which has nothing in common with the metaphysical ideal . . . of poets and orators. Geometry and poetry have their separate rules. He who undertakes to judge Homer by Euclid is no less impertinent than the one who would judge Euclid by Homer." See *Oeuvres de J. B. Rousseau* (nouvelle ed.; Paris: Lefèvre, 1830), 5:131–32.

3. As Maritain put it succinctly: "Rousseau's man is Descartes' angel, playing the beast." *Three Reformers: Luther—Descartes—Rousseau* (New York: Charles Scribner's Sons, 1929), p. 100.

4. *Confessions*, p. 17. Toward the end of his life Rousseau viewed himself as better than a saint. Unlike saints, who humbly ascribed their sufferings to their sins, Rousseau asserted that while "God wants me to suffer, He also knows that I

am innocent." *Les rêveries du promeneur solitaire,* in *Oeuvres complètes de Jean Jacques Rousseau* (Paris: Bibliothèque de la Pléiade, 1964), 1:1010.

5. See P. M. Masson, *La religion de J. J. Rousseau* (2d ed.; Paris: Hachette, 1916), 2:181–84.

6. *Rousseau juge de Jean Jacques. Dialogues,* in *Oeuvres complètes,* 1:823.

7. So Rousseau advised Msgr. de Beaumont, Archbishop of Paris, in a long letter published in 1762; *Oeuvres complètes,* 4:940.

8. *Emile,* translated by B. Foxley, with an introduction by A. B. de Monvel (London: J. M. Dent), p. 251. "Every false religion," Rousseau declared in *Julie* (IV, 10), "combats nature. Only our religion, which follows and restores nature, proclaims a dispensation which is both divine and convenient for man" *Oeuvres complètes,* 2:456.

9. *Emile,* p. 350. As to Julie, she "finds in the entire nature but occasions for emotions and gratitude." *Julie* (V, 5) in *Oeuvres complètes,* 2:591.

10. *Emile,* p. 253.

11. *Rêveries,* in *Oeuvres complètes,* 1:1047 and 1:999.

12. See Masson, *La religion de J. J. Rousseau,* vol. 2, *La "Profession de foi" de Jean-Jacques* (2d ed.; Paris: Hachette, 1916), p. 256.

13. After declaring that "the life of the soul begins with the death of the body," Rousseau continues: "But what is that life? Is the soul of man in its nature immortal? I know not." As an excuse, Rousseau refers to his inability to grasp the infinite. *Emile,* p. 246.

14. *Emile,* p. 236.

15. *Lettres morales* (à Sophie), *Oeuvres complètes,* 4:1096.

16. *A Discourse on the Origin of Inequality,* in *The Social Contract and Discourses,* translated with introduction by G. D. H. Cole (London: Dent, 1913), p. 177.

17. Ibid., p. 170.

18. "For physics may explain, in some measure, the mechanism of the sense and the formation of ideas; but in the power of willing or rather of choosing, and in the feeling of this power, nothing is to be found but acts which are purely spiritual and wholly inexplicable by the laws of mechanism"; ibid., p. 170.

19. Ibid., p. 171.

20. Letter of Aug. 30, 1755. *The Complete Works of Voltaire. Correspondence. Edition définitive.* vol. XVI (Banbury: The Voltaire Foundation, 1971), p. 258.

21. A phrase of Baumier in his apotheosis of Rousseau's tomb. See Masson, *La religion de J. J. Rousseau,* 3:76.

22. C. E. Osgood, *Method and Theory in Experimental Psychology* (New York: Oxford University Press, 1953), p. 655.

23. *Rapport du physique et du moral de l'homme,* in *Oeuvres complètes de Cabanis* (Paris: Bossange Frères, 1824), 3:159—60.

24. Ibid., 3:261–62.

25. In a glowing recension of a book by the notorious materialist, J. Moleschott, Feuerbach also stated: "Being is identical with eating; to be means to eat; what exists eats and will be eaten." See *Sämmtliche Werke* (2d ed., 1903; reprinted, Fromman Verlag Günther Holzboog, 1959), 10:14 and 22. Rousseau was clearly behind Feuerbach's phrase: *Sentio ergo sum.*

26. Reported in R. Dubos, *So Human an Animal* (New York: Charles Scribner's Sons, 1968), p. 133.

27. C. P. Snow's *Two Cultures* had very articulate antecedents even during the latter half of the 19th century, such as the debate between T. H. Huxley and Matthew Arnold on the respective merits of scientific and humanistic education. See my *Culture and Science* (Windsor, Ontario: University of Windsor Press, 1975).

28. An informative discussion, limited to the English scene, is *Ancients and Moderns: A Study of the Rise of the Scientific Movement in Seventeenth-Century England* by R. F. Jones (2d ed.; Gloucester, MA: Peter Smith, 1961). For the ramifications of the quarrel in France and for the theories it prompted concerning the rise of science, see my *The Origin of Science and the Science of Its Origin* (Edinburgh: Scottish Academic Press, 1978), especially ch. 1.

29. *Confessions*, pp. 327–28. What happened was the sudden emergence into full consciousness of an idea about primitive man, which, as Rousseau later revealed (*Dialogues*, II), had ever since his youth been at work within him as a "sentiment sourd, une notion confuse" (*Oeuvres complètes*, 1:828).

30. A point well emphasized in I. Babbitt, *Rousseau and Romanticism* (1911; New York: Meridian Books, 1955), p. 111.

31. *Confessions*, p. 329.

32. *Rêveries, Oeuvres complètes,* 1:1046.

33. "Island; or, Christian and his Comrades," Canto I, Stanza ii. The mutinous sailors of the *Bounty*, the subject of Byron's long poem, "preferred the cave of some soft savage" (ibid), one of the many phrases that conjure up Rousseau.

34. Passages from this essay will be quoted from its English translation, *A Discourse on the Moral Effects of the Arts and Sciences*, in *The Social Contract and Other Discourses*, (see n16, above), pp. 117–42.

35. Ibid., p. 120.

36. Ibid., pp. 124–25. Rousseau's remarks were as extremist as the position of most 18th-century sinophiles, among whom Voltaire was a leader. For a discussion of more balanced contemporary views, see my *The Origin of Science and the Science of Its Origin*, ch. 2.

37. Ibid., p. 131.

38. Ibid., p. 132.

39. Ibid., p. 140.

40. Rousseau cited Bacon, Descartes, and Newton (p. 141). Descartes and Newton had proper training. As to Bacon, he too had some, though not as much as Oxford could offer in the 1580s. That Bacon appeared to Rousseau as one well versed in the sciences was a fallacy which Rousseau shared with d'Alembert, Diderot, Voltaire, and other leaders of the Enlightenment.

41. See *Confessions*, pp. 221 and 226.

42. "Let him not be taught science, let him discover it" (*Emile*, p. 131). The science of the day, Rousseau declared on the first page of *Emile*, tended "rather to destroy than to build up."

43. *Emile*, p. 167.

44. "Supplément au voyage de Bougainville," in *Diderot Oeuvres complètes* (Paris: Le Club Français du Livre, 1971), 10:245–46. In the same context Diderot also spoke, again echoing Rousseau, "of the extreme circumstances which lead man back to his primitive simplicity."

45. *Reflections on the Revolution in France*, edited with an introduction by C. C. O'Brien (Harmondsworth: Penguin Books, 1968), p. 187.

46. In a letter to Innes, May 29, 1871; see *The Life and Letters of Charles Darwin*, ed. F. Darwin (London: J. Murray, 1888), 3:140.

47. *Materialism and Empirio-criticism: Critical Comments on a Reactionary Philosophy* (New York: International Publishers, 1927), p. 211. Lenin merely echoed an early Marxist, E. Aveling. See G. Himmelfarb, *Darwin and the Darwinian Revolution* (New York: W. W. Norton, 1962), p. 387.

48. Only a reader with little philosophical sensitivity could be impressed by the reference in *Charles Darwin and the Problem of Creation* (Chicago: University of Chicago Press, 1979) by N. C. Gillespie, to epistemology as the ultimate issue between Christianity and Darwinism (pp. 149–52). It is hardly philosophical to quote J. S. Mill as a peremptory witness for the impossibility of knowing miracles and not to recall the epistemological basis of that impossibility as specified by Mill. On that basis not only miracles are impossible but also the cultivation of science insofar as it assumes the possibility of knowing a fully consistent and contingent universe. For Mill, external material reality is merely the permanent possibility of sensations. He finds nothing contradictory in the possibility of a universe in which two and two do not make four. Such a remark, which I have developed at length in my Gifford Lectures, *The Road of Science and the Ways to God* (Chicago: University of Chicago Press, 1978), is of course meaningless within the framework of Kuhnian paradigms, the ultimate tribunal for Gillespie. There the final verdict lies not with epistemology but with paradigms as mere sociological and psychological phenomena. It was no accident that Kuhn himself made recourse to Darwinism as the highest forum, a move which forced him, and all his disciples, to cast their lot with circularity in reasoning. Such is the logic of any reasoning which ultimately is not an epistēmē properly so called.

49. References will be to the published text in *Darwin on Man: A Psychological Study of Scientific Creativity*, by H. E. Gruber, together with *Darwin's Early and Unpublished Notebooks*, transcribed and annotated by P. H. Barrett, with a foreword by J. Piaget (New York: E. P. Dutton & Co., 1974). The notebooks date from the period 1837–39 and are identified by various capital letters. Gruber, himself a materialist, provides ample evidence that creativity, scientific or other, far surpasses the limits of a psychology steeped in materialism.

50. This is why many pages are missing from the notebooks.

51. "Thinking consists of sensation of images before your eyes, or ears, . . . or of memory of such sensation, & memory is repetition of whatever takes place in brain, when sensation is perceived." (M notebook, p. 277). One wonders how thought could indicate anything wondrous to one who wrote: "People often talk of the wonderful event of intellectual man appearing.—the appearance of insects with other sense is more wonderful" (B notebook, p. 446).

52. M notebook, p. 278.

53. N notebook, p. 333.

54. C notebook, p. 451. References to man's arrogance are a staple feature of the notebooks. Their tendentiousness, to say nothing of their naiveté, is well exemplified in the following statement: "Let man visit Ourang-outang in domestication, hear expressive whine, see its intelligence when spoken [to], as if understood every word said . . . let him look at savage, roasting his parent, naked, artless, not improving, yet improvable" (C notebook, p. 449). Was not the savage, for all his cruelty, far superior to the orang-outang, precisely because the latter was in all evidence, not improvable?

55. N notebook, p. 33.

56. M notebook, p. 276.

57. C notebook, p. 450.

58. Marx and his followers advocated less patient methods for bringing about the age of "scientific thought." Darwin's letter to E. Aveling written in 1880, is quoted in *Darwin Revalued*, by Sir Arthur Keith (London: Watts, 1955), p. 234, where erroneously Marx is named as its recipient.

59. B notebook, p. 446 and M notebook, p. 289.

60. *The Old Faith and the New: A Confession by David Friedrich Strauss*, translated by M. Blind (New York: Henry Holt, 1873), 1:204–05.

61. "Cosmic Emotion," in *Lectures and Essays*, edited by L. Stephen and F. Pollock (London: Macmillan, 1901), 2:297.

62. "The Ethics of Religion," ibid., 2:245.

63. Ibid., 2:243–44.

64. G. Bradford, *Darwin* (Boston: Houghton Mifflin Company, 1926), p. 245.

65. In his letter of July 3, 1881, to W. Graham, in *The Life and Letters of Charles Darwin*, 1:316.

66. In his foreword to *Darwin's Theory Applied to Mankind* by A. Machin (London: Longmans, Green and Co., 1937), p. viii.

67. *The Descent of Man and Selection in Relation to Sex* (new ed.; London: John Murray, 1901), p. 931.

68. Ibid., p. 194.

69. J. Martineau, "Nature and God" (1860), in *Essays, Reviews and Addresses* (London: Longmans, Green and Co., 1891), 3:160.

70. *The Everlasting Man* (1925; Garden City, N.Y.: Doubleday, 1955), p. 13.

71. *What Is Wrong with the World?* (New York: Dodd, Mead and Co., 1910), pp. 325–26.

72. In his letter of July 11, 1861, to W. Graham, in *Life and Letters*, 1:316.

73. *An Autobiography* (New York: D. Appleton, 1904), 2:548–49.

74. In his letter of May 22, 1860, to A. Gray, in *Life and Letters*, 1:312.

75. *The Autobiography of Charles Darwin*, with original omissions restored, edited with appendix and notes by his granddaughter, Nora Barlow (New York: W. W. Norton, 1969), p. 140.

76. In an unsigned review, "Geological Climates and the Origin of Species," of two books by Sir Charles Lyell, in *The Quarterly Review*, 126 (1869): 359–94; see especially p. 392.

77. "With the Hominids the same increase [doubling of the brain] seems to have taken place, geologically speaking, in an instant without having been accompanied by a major increase in size," declared T. Edinger at the International Colloquium on Paleontology, held in Paris, April 1955. See his address, "Objets et résultats de la paléoneurologie," *Annales de paléoneurologie* 42 (1956): 99.

78. S. J. Gould, *Ever since Darwin: Reflections in Natural History* (New York: W. W. Norton, 1977), pp. 184–85.

79. *Aspects of Theory of Syntax* (Cambridge, MA: MIT Press, 1965), p. 58. More recently Chomsky remarked: "It's about as likely that an ape will prove to have a language ability as that there is an island somewhere with a species of flightless birds waiting for human beings to teach them to fly." Quoted in *Time*, March 10, 1980, p. 57. Such recent books as *Nim* by H. Terrace (New York: Knopf, 1979) and the collection of essays, *Speaking of Apes* (New York: Plenum, 1980), sufficiently exposed the lack of rigor in reports on experiments aimed at proving the existence of language ability in apes.

80. A very recent case is the claim of B. F. Skinner and his two co-workers that behavioral conditioning is the means by which not only men, but also apes and

pigeons learn the art of symbolic communication, that is, language. See R. Epstein, R. P. Lanza and B. F. Skinner, "Symbolic Communication between Two Pigeons," *Science,* 207 (1980): 543—45.

81. For details, see my *The Relevance of Physics* (Chicago: University of Chicago Press, 1966), pp. 301—05. The prospect of vast amounts of time is still the ultimate appeal of Darwinists. A very recent example is in *Lucy* (see n83 below) where one is also given a classic evidence of the ease with which "the gentle flow of . . . a lot of time" dispenses even with the physical (ontological) trigger to start something new. No less revealing is the assertion made in the same breath: "You also have pretty smart animals. They can try things. Not in the sense that they say to themselves, "Wow, we're bipedal, we've got a free hand, let's take some lunch home to the little lady.' It's nothing like that. No animal is ever remotely conscious of the evolutionary processes it is undergoing. Those take place in tiny increments" (p. 335). Such and innumerable other passages in Darwinist writings should give a field-day to any logician. Lucy's erect posture raises its specific problems when taken as the basis for drawing the family tree of anthropoids. The old age of that fossil demands a diagram (see p. 365) in which man appears as isolated as ever.

82. Vol. XIV, p. 763.

83. Reported in *Newsweek*, January 29, 1979, p. 81. Leakey's dissent is part of the voice, usually ignored, of a most respectable minority among Darwinian evolutionists who refuse to blind themselves to the shortcomings of evidence. The endurance, over four generations, of a group of strong dissenters within a scientific school, such as Darwinism, is unique in the history of modern science. The question of "missing link" is only one of several salient topics concerning Darwinian evolution where the voice of dissent does not die out. Another is the eye, human or animal, which provokes time and again profound doubts in leading evolutionists whether it can really be the outcome of mere chance. Presentation in case histories of such dissent would well repay the effort. Leakey's dissent is registered with obvious slants in *Lucy: The Beginnings of Humankind*, written by D. C. Johanson, the discoverer of "Lucy," and M. A. Edey (New York: Simon and Schuster, 1981), pp. 298–300.

84. Quoted in *Patterns in Prehistory*, by R. J. Wenke (New York: Oxford University Press, 1980), p. 163.

85. R. E. Leakey and R. Lewin, *People of the Lake: Mankind and Its Beginnings* (Garden City, N.Y.: Doubleday, 1978).

86. Delivered by Philipp Morrison at the Massachussetts Institute of Technology for BBC Television and Radio. For its text, see *The Listener*, August 23, 1979, pp. 234—38.

87. "Never use the word higher and lower," wrote Darwin on a slip of paper which he kept inserted in his copy of Chambers's *Vestiges of the Natural History of Creation*. See *More Letters of Charles Darwin: A Record of His Work in a Series of Hitherto Unpublished Letters*, ed. F. Darwin and A. C. Seward (New York: D. Appleton, 1903), 1:114.

88. H. Drummond's *The Ascent of Man* (London: Hodder and Stoughton, 1894) was a better book in the sense that Drummond refused to reduce love to any form of struggle for life. While in the final analysis Drummond was a reductionist, he at least recognized the problem by positing two basic biological forces, evidenced in nutrition and procreation respectively: "One begets competition, self-assertion, war; the other unselfishness, self-effacement, peace. One is Individualism, the other, Altruism" (p. 25).

89. *Evolution and Ethics and Other Essays* (New York: D. Appleton, 1914), pp. 81–82.

90. *The Autobiography of Charles Darwin*, pp. 94–95. The concluding page of *The Descent* contains the same contradictory view.

91. *Sociobiology: The New Synthesis* (Cambridge, MA: The Belknap Press of Harvard University Press, 1975), p. 3.

92. *The Descent of Man*, p. 946.

93. *Evolution and Ethics*, p. 81.

94. "Biogenesis and Abiogenesis" (1870), in *Discourses: Biological and Geological* (London: Macmillan, 1894), pp. 256–57.

95. L. Huxley, *The Life and Letters of Thomas Henry Huxley* (London: Macmillan, 1900), 1:263.

96. *A New Dictionary of Quotations on Historical Principles from Ancient and Modern Sources*, selected and edited by H. L. Mencken (New York: Alfred A. Knopf, 1946), p. 790.

97. "A Free Man's Worship" (1903), in *Mysticism and Logic* (Garden City, NY.: Doubleday, 1957), p. 45.

98. The occasion, the 50th anniversary in 1943 of T. H. Huxley's Romanes Lecture, could not have been more appropriate. It was no less appropriate for a Darwinian philosopher such as Julian Huxley to entangle himself in a self-defeating fallacy from the very start. For if it were true that the dilemma which T. H. Huxley found unresolvable could be resolved by considering ethics not as a fixed entity but as part of the all-encompassing evolution of the "world-stuff," then nothing could be exempt from the absence of fixity, not even the "intellectual tool . . . of developmental analysis" or the "insight" allegedly provided by it, to say nothing of the mechanism of evolution. See "Evolutionary Ethics" in *Touchstone for Ethics* by T. H. Huxley and Julian Huxley (New York: Harper and Brothers, 1947), p. 116. The grandfather, in all likelihood, would have spiritedly disagreed with the grandson who attributed the old gentleman's viewing the dilemma as unresolvable to his inability to rid himself completely of his youthful upbringing in a Christian tradition for which ethics is essentially a fixed entity.

99. *Nature*, 173 (1954), pp. 227 and 279.

100. He did so in his Romanes Lecture, quoted above.

101. These themes were extensively documented in my *Science and Creation: From Eternal Cycles to an Oscillating Universe* (Edinburgh: Scottish Academic Press, 1974).

102. The statement in the *Descent* (p. 92) is important here. It reveals that public debate forced Darwin to make public a view (which he had already expressed in a letter to Asa Gray in 1863), that the overthrow of the idea of special creation of any species was much more important for him than the verification of natural selection as *the* mechanism of evolution. The debate turned on the point whether evolution and Creation were compatible. One could only wish that Darwin had publicly repudiated the reference to the Creator at the end of the first edition of the *Origin*. The reference was not to special creation but to a primordial creative act leaving a free course to the subsequent evolution of any and all. It was only in private that Darwin spoke of his regret that in that first edition he had "truckled to public opinion." See his letter of March 29, 1863, to J. D. Hooker in *The Life and Letters of Charles Darwin*, edited by F. Darwin (London: J. Murray, 1888), 3:18.

103. *The Descent of Man*, pp. 72–73.

104. W. Irvine, *Apes, Angels, and Victorians: Darwin, Huxley, and Evolution* (New York: McGraw Hill, 1955), p. 196.

105. *The Descent of Man*, p. 927.

106. *Ends and Means: An Enquiry into the Nature of Ideals and into the Kinds of Methods Employed for Their Realization* (London: Chatto and Windus, 1937), p. 274. On Huxley's acknowledgment of erotic motivations at work on behalf of Darwinism, see pp. 267 and 269.

107. As distinct from what Huxley called "the easy-going philosophy of general meaninglessness" (ibid., p. 274).

108. According to E. Gilson, *D'Aristôte à Darwin et retour* (Paris: J. Vrin, 1971, p. 49), Claude Bernard declined to answer questions about his opinion on life on the ground that he had not encountered life as such.

109. While the last chapter of Wilson's *Sociobiology* (see note 91 above) was revealing enough in its sudden and obviously unjustified jump from ants to man, the advocacy of materialism on behalf of evolutionism was brazen in Wilson's *On Human Nature:* "The core of scientific materialism is the evolutionary epic . . . the evolutionary epic is probably the best myth we will ever have. It can be adjusted until it comes as close to truth as the human mind is constructed to judge the truth. And if that is the case, the mythopoeic requirements of the mind must somehow be met by scientific materialism so as to reinvest our superb energies" (Cambridge, MA: Harvard University Press, 1978, p. 209).

110. *Genes, Mind and Culture: The Coevolutionary Process* (Cambridge, MA, Harvard University Press, 1981), p. 295.

111. *The Descent of Man*, p. 4.

112. *Heartbreak House* (London: Constable, 1919), p. xiii.

113. In contrast to, for example, the *Encyclopaedia Universalis* (Paris: Encyclopaedia Universalis France S.A.) which not only contains a long article "L' homme" (vol. 8 [1968], pp. 501—26) but has as its first subdivision a survey of philosophical considerations on man's nature from the Greeks to the present times.

114. *Thus Spake Zarathustra*, translated by T. Common (New York: Macmillan, 1916), p. 7. The chief reason for this was man's reluctance to turn into a Superman. By assigning to man such lofty goal, Nietzsche contradicted himself as he also declared in the same Prologue: "Man is a rope stretched between the animal and the Superman—a rope over an abyss . . . . What is great in man is that he is a bridge and not a goal" (p. 9).

Chapter Three

1. *Antigone*, 332–33. Actually, the chorus sings man's praises because of his conquest of the forces of nature.

2. The second part of Protagoras' dictum, hardly ever quoted, "of the things that are, that they are, and of the tings that are not, that they are not," reveals strongly that solipsism which bars even the possibility of wonderment. Probably the first part of Protagoras' dictum would be less popular if quoted in the more correct translation as "man is the measurer of all things."

3. See D. J. De Solla Price, *Science since Babylon* (New Haven: Yale University Press, 1961), p. 107, where data are given on behalf of the estimate that between 80 and 90 percent of all those who could be looked upon as scientists, were alive in the middle of the 20th century.

4. For further details about the explosive increase in the resolving power of various scientific instruments, see ch. 6, "The Edge of Precision," in my *The Relevance of Physics* (Chicago: University of Chicago Press, 1966).

5. Accelerators were not even twenty years old when the exponential growth of their maximum energies was noted. See D. J. De Solla Price, *Little Science, Big Science* (New York: Columbia University Press, 1963), p. 27.

6. For details and diagram, see ch. 8, "The Myth of One Island," in my *The Milky Way: An Elusive Road for Science* (New York: Science History Publications, 1972).

7. Although the subordinate status of spiral galaxies had already been vigorously challenged prior to January 1, 1925, Hubble's report on that day to the Astronomical Society of Washington about the true distance of Andromeda was dramatic. See *The Milky Way*, pp. 301–02.

8. "A Relation between Distance and Radial Velocity among Extra-galactic Nebulae," *Proceedings of the National Academy of Sciences* (Washington, D.C.), 15 (1929) :173.

9. See *Time*, February 9, 1981, p. 46, and L. Spitzer, Jr., "The Space Telescope," *American Scientist*, 66 (1978): 426–31.

10. A theme developed in detail in chs. 4 and 5, "The Layers of Matter," and "The Frontiers of the Cosmos," in my *The Relevance of Physics* (cited in n4, above).

11. Less remembered is the continuation of that *pensée*: "All our dignity consists, then, in thought." See *Pascal's Pensées*, translated by W. F. Trotter, with an introduction by T. S. Eliot (New York: E. P. Dutton, 1958), p. 97 (No. 347).

12. A new garb given by Herbert Feigl and his school to a now rather old shoe, logical positivism.

13. Such a definition of the universe should seem an elementary dictate of rigorous thinking and is certainly demanded by the practice of science. That it cannot readily be evaded is amply illustrated by the verbal exertions of William James in his *A Pluralistic Universe* (London: Longmans, Green and Co., 1909), pp. 324–28.

14. A sheer verbalization aimed at avoiding the necessity of facing up to the real content of any and all universals.

15. The figure is close to zero, which is the curvature of a Euclidean universe.

16. See E. Borel, *Space and Time* (London: Blackie & Son, 1926), pp. 226–27.

17. For its English translation, "Cosmological Considerations on the General Theory of Relativity," see *The Principle of Relativity: A Collection of Original Memoirs on the Special and General Theory of Relativity*, by H. A. Lorentz, A. Einstein, H. Minkowksi and H. Weyl, with notes by A. Sommerfeld, translated by W. Perett and G. B. Jeffrey (1923; New York: Dover, n.d.), pp. 177–88.

18. Space, or the net of permissible paths of motion will in that case resemble a saddle with no edges.

19. For details on some early estimates, see *The Relevance of Physics*, p. 227.

20. See note 17 above.

21. He did so in 1927 in an article published in a Belgian periodical. It gained world-wide attention four years later when published in English translation in the *Monthly Notices of the Royal Astronomical Society*, 91 (1931): 483–90.

22. Such was the thrust, for instance, of the papers read by Jeans and Millikan at a panel on the evolution of the universe held as part of the centennial meeting of the British Association for the Advancement of Science in London, late September, 1931. For details, see my *Cosmos and Creator* (Edinburgh: Scottish Academic Press, 1981), pp. 7–14.

23. Documentary evidence in this respect is available in the last chapter, "Oscillating Worlds and Wavering Minds," in my *Science and Creation: From Eternal Cycles to an Oscillating Universe* (Edinburgh: Scottish Academic Press, 1974). For more recent details, see my paper, "The History of Science and the Idea of an Oscillating Universe," in *Cosmology, History and Theology* edited by W. Yourgrau and A. D. Breck (New York: Plenum Press, 1977), pp. 233–52.

24. R. C. Tolman, *Relativity, Thermodynamics and Cosmology* (Oxford: Clarendon Press, 1934), p. 443. The ignoring of that diagram is all the more curious in view of the fact that Tolman's massive work has since been reprinted at least half-a-dozen times. More recently, the diagram, in a somewhat different form, was given new publicity through *The Physics of Time Assymmetry* by P. C. W. Davies (Berkeley: University of California Press, 1974), p. 191.

25. Only a consideration of metaphysical, or rather countermetaphysical postulates can explain the popularity which the steady-state theory enjoyed from its original formulation in 1948 until the mid-sixties, and in some circles even beyond. The emergence of new hydrogen atoms at a steady rate everywhere in the universe *out of nothing* was clearly a claim which only committed materialists would entertain. As to the christening, by Bondi, Gold, and Hoyle, of their basic postulate as "perfect cosmological principle," it could seem an innocent phrase only to those unaware of the age-old resolve of materialists to see in the universe a "perfect" entity. Adepts of the steady-state theory hardly concern themselves with that infinite matter that must pile up beyond the observable limits of the universe. Evidently they envision that infinity of matter passing quite as conveniently and causelessly out of existence as it passed in.

26. Dicke and his co-workers at Princeton had just completed an apparatus to detect that radiation, first postulated by Gamow in 1934, when they received a telephone call from Penzias and Wilson about a strange residual noise in their large horn antenna, a noise which turned out to be caused, in fact, by that cosmic background radiation. See R. H. Dicke, *Gravitation and the Universe* (Philadelphia: American Philosophical Society, 1970), p. 66.

27. The cosmic background radiation can only be explained as the result of a highly condensed state of *all* matter, which is inadmissible within the steady-state theory. The proof of that highly condensed state consists in the fact that the radiation in question has the characteristics of a so-called black-body radiation.

28. In the spring of 1974, for instance, following the presentation of a paper by Princeton astrophysicist J. P. Ostriker before the American Physical Society in Chicago, newsreports glowed with satisfaction at the discovery of the "missing mass" in halos surrounding galaxies—a claim that proved to be unfounded.

29. On the significance of the "missing mass" for astrophysicists of dialectical materialist persuasion, see *Science*, 211 (1981): 472.

30. A book by S. Weinberg, first published in 1977 (London: André Deutsch).

31. The question of creation out of nothing is carefully sidestepped by Weinberg. See, for instance, p. 149.

32. Mainly concerned with the formation of chemical elements and of nuclei. The formation of galaxies is still a largely unresolved problem, but relatively minor compared with the former topic.

33. Ibid., pp. 104–05. For somewhat different data, see B. Lovell: *In the Centre of Immensities* (London: Hutchinson, 1979), pp. 99–105.

34. For an early statement, see B. Carter, "Large Number Coincidences and the Anthropic Principle in Cosmology," in M. S. Longair (ed.), *Confrontation of Cosmological Theories with Observational Data* (Dordrecht: D. Reidel, 1974), pp. 291–98. A graphic and concise way of stating the anthropic principle is the remark, "God made the fine structure constant to be 1/137, so that we would arise to worship Him," attributed to a prominent physicist by the science reporter, D. E. Thomsen, in "The Universe: Chaotic or Bioselective?" *Science News*, 106 (1975): 124.

35. For details, see S. Weinberg, *The First Three Minutes*, pp. 133–49; or, P. Davies, *The Runaway Universe* (New York: Harper & Row, 1978), pp. 42–50.

36. Their reaction can easily be understood if one recalls that cosmos and cosmology are seen instinctively as the citadel of theism even by those who did not read J. S. Mill's *Autobiography* (see n46 below).

37. *The Philosophy of Physical Science* (New York: Macmillan, 1939), p. 109.

38. For a very readable account of the background, genesis, and success of Eddington's *Fundamental Theory*, published posthumously in 1946, see A. V. Douglas, *The Life of Arthur Stanley Eddington* (London: Thomas Nelson, 1957), pp. 145–82.

39. In Eddington's words, "that queer quantity 'infinity' is the very mischief and no rational physicist should have anything to do with it." *New Pathways in Science* (Cambridge: University Press, 1934), p. 217.

40. Einstein's concise formulation of the infinity of gravitational potential at any point in an infinite homogeneous universe, given in a footnote of his *Relativity: The Special and General Theory* (first published in 1917; New York: Crown Publishers, 1961, p. 106), is different only in notation from the one given by Lord Kelvin in 1901. For the history of the problem, see my article, "Das Gravitations-Paradoxon des unendlichen Universums," in *Südhoffs Archiv*, 63 (1979) :105–22.

41. For documentation on this and subsequent details in this paragraph, see my *The Paradox of Olbers' Paradox: A Case History of Scientific Thought* (New York: Herder & Herder, 1969).

42. See the English translation of Riemann's lecture, "On the Hypotheses which Lie at the Bases of Geometry," in *Mathematical Papers by William Kingdon Clifford*, edited by Robert Tucker, with an introduction by H. J. S. Smith (London: Macmillan, 1882), pp. 55–69; for quotation, see p. 69.

43. See the chapter on the finiteness of matter in endless space in Zöllner's monograph on the nature of comets, *Ueber die Natur der Cometen: Beiträge zur Geschichte und Theorie der Erkenntnis* (Leipzig: Wilhelm Engelmann, 1872), pp. 299–312. For a discussion, see my *The Paradox of Olbers' Paradox*, pp. 158–62.

44. The context was a series of lectures, delivered in March 1873, on the philosophy of pure sciences. See W. K. Clifford, *Lectures and Essays*, edited by L. Stephen and F. Pollock (London: Macmillan, 1901), 1:386–87.

45. J. S. Mill, *Examination of Sir William Hamilton's Philosophy and of the Principal Philosophical Questions Discussed in His Writings* (6th ed.; London: Longmans, Green and Co., 1889), p. 233.

46. *Autobiography of John Stuart Mill*, published for the first time without alterations and omissions from the original manuscript in the possession of Columbia University, with a preface by John Jacob Coss (New York: Columbia University Press, 1924), p. 158.

47. See Helmholtz's address delivered in 1870 "On the Origin and Significance of Geometrical Axioms," a criticism of Kant's *Metaphysical Foundations of Natural Science* in *Popular Scientific Lectures*, edited by M. Kline (New York: Dover, 1962), pp. 223—49. The same point was made by Gauss to the older Bolyai in a letter written on March 6, 1832, but published only in 1898.

48. Although some time before Weierstrass gave his inaugural lecture, in 1857, some mathematicians, such as Sophus Lie, the father of group theory, pursued their work with no concern for possible application in physics, that lecture may be considered as the programmatic start of the emancipation of mathematics from physics. For details, see my *The Relevance of Physics*, pp. 116–17.

49. A fact which prompted the title of E. P. Wigner's memorable lecture, "The Unreasonable Effectiveness of Mathematics in the Natural Sciences," *Communications on Pure and Applied Mathematics*, 13 (1960): 1–14.

50. Gödel did so in November, 1930, in a paper read before the Austrian Academy of Sciences.

51. Ironically, a month later, in December 1930, Hilbert assured the Philosophical Society of Hamburg that ultimate certainty can be achieved in number theory, the fundamental branch of mathematics. For details, see *The Relevance of Physics*, p. 127.

52. "Mathematics and Logic," *American Mathematical Monthly*, 53 (1946) : 13.

53. Their statements to that effect are quoted in my *Cosmos and Creator* (Edinburgh: Scottish Academic Press, 1981), pp. 45–47.

54. This elementary feat was first accomplished in 1966, in my *The Relevance of Physics*, pp. 127–30.

55. On October 7, 1976, Professor Murray Gell-Mann gave assurance in such a vein before an audience of over two thousand at the Twelfth Nobel Conference, Gustavus Adolphus College, St. Peter, Minnesota.

56. Translated by Arnold Rosin (New York: Viking Press, 1977), p. v.

57. Therein lies also the source of the basic inadequacy of Piaget's system. As succinctly put in a major study of his work: "It is not of course surprising that the symbolic should prove a difficulty for a naturalistic theory of man—Piaget's or any other. Naturalistic theories make sense only if they can contain man as a phenomenon—describe and understand his thought in its symbolic complexity—within an evolutionary perspective. There is little evidence that this can be done." B. Rotman, *Jean Piaget: Psychologist of the Real* (Ithaca, N.Y.: Cornell University Press, 1977), p. 180.

58. 1 Cor 1:17.

59. Rom 1:18–21.

60. 1 Thess 4:14, 1 Cor 15:51. Christ Himself said of the dead Lazarus that he was merely asleep, Jn 11:12.

61. Saint Paul in fact insisted that Christian stewardship ought to be a *logike*

latreia (Rom 12:1) by which he meant the full use of reason, hardly evident in the mere logic-chopping cultivated, for example, by logical positivists.

62. As is evidenced by the post-Kantian history of philosophy, once these three are recognized as valid notions, knowledge can again be liberated from the confines of the merely sensory, which otherwise remains the prison-house of reason.

63. The "drudgery" with which modern scholarship renders the Vulgate's "militia" (military service) in Jb 7:1 (see also Jb 14:14) is etymologically related to the latter. At any rate, the idea that Christian life must imply the tenaciousness of military service is all too clearly emphasized by Saint Paul.

64. Perhaps not for some privileged members of the affluent society and for some academics withdrawn to their ivory tower, but certainly to an overwhelming majority of mankind, plagued with disease, hunger, and war, and in large part because of the technological abuses of science.

65. Unfortunately, the statement has gained wide currency within the Christian camp through the poetic flights of Teilhard de Chardin.

66. For a documentation of young Einstein's admiration for Ostwald, Mach, and Kant, see G. Holton, "Mach, Einstein, and the Search for Reality" (1968), in Holton, *Thematic Origins of Scientific Thought: Kepler to Einstein* (Cambridge, MA: Harvard University Press, 1973), pp. 219–25.

67. "Ernst Mach," *Physikalische Zeitschrift*, 17 (1916): 101–04. When ten years later young Heisenberg reminded Einstein of the "Machist" reasoning in his writings on special relativity, Einstein replied: "Possibly I did use this kind of reasoning, but it is nonsense all the same." See W. Heisenberg, *Physics and Beyond* (New York: Harper and Row, 1971), p. 63.

68. While E. T. Whittaker may be faulted for giving but a brief mention to Einstein in his discussion of special relativity in his classic work, *A History of the Theories of Aether and Electricity. Volume Two: The Modern Theories 1900 –1926* (London: Thomas Nelson, 1953; see ch. 2, "The Relativity Theory of Poincaré and Lorentz"), much greater is the fault of those who in their uncritical admiration for Einstein assign to him the lion's share of credit in that respect.

69. Einstein's letter of September 30, 1921 to E. Zschimmer is quoted in G. Holton, "Einstein's Scientific Program: The Formative Years," in H. Woolf (ed.), *Some Strangeness in the Proportion* (New York: Addison-Wesley, 1980), p. 63.

70. For further development of that theme, see my paper, "The Absolute beneath the Relative: Reflections on Einstein's Theories," read at the Einstein Memorial Symposium held in November 1979 at Hofstra University, to be published soon.

71. Thus P. G. Bergmann spoke of the "breakdown of the principle of relativity [with respect] to the background radiation" in his "Cosmology as a Science," in R. J. Seeger and R. S. Cohen (eds.), *Philosophical Foundations of Science* (Dordrecht: D. Reidel, 1974), p. 185.

72. *Bulletin de la Société Française de Philosophie*, 17 (1922): 101.

73. P. Frank, *Einstein: His Life and Times* (New York: A. Knopf, 1947), p. 213.

74. Quoted in Holton, "Mach, Einstein and the Search for Reality," p. 243.

75. *The World as I See It* (New York: Covici-Friede, 1934), p. 60.

76. "Without belief that it is possible to grasp the reality with our theoretical constructions, without the belief in the inner harmony of our world, there could be no science. This belief is and always will remain the fundamental motive for all scientific creation." *The Evolution of Physics* (New York: Simon and Schuster, 1938), p. 313.

77. "Remarks on Bertrand Russell's Theory of Knowledge," in P. A. Schilpp (ed.), *The Philosophy of Bertrand Russell* (La Salle, IL: Open Court Publishing Company: Library of Living Philosophers, 1946), p. 289.

78. "Autobiographical Notes, in P. A. Schilpp, *Albert Einstein: Philosopher-Scientist* (La Salle, IL: Open Court Publishing Company, 1949, & New York: Harper Torchbooks, 1959), p. 673.

79. Argued in further detail in my *The Road of Science and the Ways to God* (Chicago: University of Chicago Press, 1978), p. 209.

80. The moment of truth for Einstein did not come until he read a paper by Mach, written in 1913 but only published six years after Mach's death, in which Mach rejected relativity because he sensed the metaphysical content in it.

81. *Letters on Wave Mechanics: Schrödinger, Planck, Einstein, Lorentz*, edited by K. Przibram, translated with an introduction by M. Klein (New York: Philosophical Library, 1967), p. 36.

82. Einstein's letter of December 3, 1953, to M. Born in *The Born-Einstein Letters. Correspondence between Albert Einstein and Max and Hedwig Born from 1916 to 1955 with commentaries by Max Born*, translated by Irene Born (New York: Walker and Company, 1971), p. 209.

83. Pauli's letter of March 31, 1954, to Born, ibid., p. 223.

84. *Out of My Later Years* (New York: Philosophical Library, 1950), p. 59.

85. *The Philosophy of Physical Science* (New York: Macmillan Company, 1939), p. 77.

86. See ch. 1, "Réalisme et sens commun," in Etienne Gilson, *Réalisme Thomiste et critique de la connaissance* (Paris: J. Vrin, 1939).

87. Letter of March 30, 1952, to M. Solovine, in *Lettres à Maurice Solovine* (Paris: Gauthier-Villars, 1956), p. 104.

88. Ibid. Einstein felt he had to assure on this point his life-long friend lest he should think that he (Einstein) "had fallen into the hands of priests."

89. *Out of My Later Years*, pp. 60–61.

90. Quoted in Holton, "Mach, Einstein, and the Search for Reality," p. 237.

91. Quoted in Holton's review of Clark's *Einstein: The Life and Times*, in *New York Times Book Review*, Sept. 5, 1971, p. 20. col. 2. See also B. Hoffmann, *Albert Einstein: Creator and Rebel*, with the collaboration of Helen Dukas (New York: The Viking Press, 1972), p. 224 and 228, for similar statements. In 1929 Einstein wrote: "Once one assumes the basic hypotheses of molecular kinetic theory, one realizes in a sense that God himself could not have established those connections other than as they actually exist." See his contribution to *Festschrift Prof. Dr. A. Stodola überreicht* (Zurich: Orell Füssli, 1929), p. 127.

92. *The World as I See It*, p. 80.

93. A personal recollection of H. Feigl from 1920. See his "Beyond Peaceful Coexistence," in R. H. Stuewer (ed.), *Historical and Philosophical Perspectives of Science* (Minneapolis: University of Minnesota Press, 1970), p. 9.

94. See, for instance, T. S. Kuhn, *The Structure of Scientific Revolutions* (Chicago: University of Chicago Press, 1962), pp. 171–72 and S. Toulmin, "The Evolutionary Development of Natural Science," *American Scientist*, 55 (1967): 456–71.

95. This recognition is hardly new and had to be reached even apart from Rousseau by any intellectual not mindful of the dignity of intellect. Taine, a Darwinist, displayed a remarkable logic in commenting on his doubts, which enveloped him toward the end of his life, concerning the value of his life-long research on history

and human intellect: "Il est possible que la vérité scientifique soit au fond malsaine pour l'animal humain tel qu'il est fait."

96. A Bulgarian proverb, quoted in *The Faber Book of Aphorisms*, edited by W. H. Auden and L. Kronenberger (London: Faber and Faber, 1964), p. 255.

97. G. E. Buckle, *The Life of Benjamin Disraeli, Earl of Beaconsfield, Vol. IV, 1855–1868* (New York: Macmillan, 1916), p. 374. The speech was delivered at the invitation of Bishop Wilberforce to an overflow audience at a diocesan meeting in Oxford on November 24, 1864.

98. S. Weinberg, *The First Three Minutes*, p. 154.

"Man is an intellectual animal and therefore an everlasting contradiction to himself. His senses center in himself, his ideas reach to the end of the universe; so that he is torn in pieces between the two, without a possibility of its ever being otherwise. A mere physical being, or a pure spirit, can alone be satisfied with itself."

—William Hazlitt, *Characteristics*, CLVIII

INDEX

128

From the same publisher: